HISTORICAL RECORDS AND STUDIES

UNITED STATES CATHOLIC HISTORICAL SOCIETY

MONOGRAPH SERIES XXV

———

ANDRÉS PÉREZ DE RIBAS

Pioneer Black Robe of the West Coast, Administrator, Historian

by

PETER MASTEN DUNNE, S.J., Ph.D.

University of San Francisco

Edited by

JOHN J. MENG

NEW YORK
THE UNITED STATES CATHOLIC
HISTORICAL SOCIETY
1951

Copyright 1951
THE UNITED STATES CATHOLIC
HISTORICAL SOCIETY

Editor of Publications
JOHN J. MENG, PH.D.

Publications Committee
JOHN J. MENG, PH.D.

A. PAUL LEVACK, PH.D.   RICHARD REID, LITT.D.

OFFICE OF
THE EXECUTIVE SECRETARY OF THE SOCIETY
SUITE 103
924 WEST END AVENUE, NEW YORK 25, NEW YORK

FOREWORD

The brilliant tapestry of United States history is woven of many threads. The design of the whole is apparent in broad sweeps to the casual observer. Yet understanding of the details of the design requires the analysis of the trained historian. Without this analysis we can never hope thoroughly to understand our cultural heritage. This fact was recognized in the 1880's by the formation of a number of organizations of professional historians dedicated to the study of the history of our country in all its details. This Society was one of these pioneer groups.

Vast portions of our nation trace their beginnings back to activities in which the Church and its members played decisive rôles. To this Catholic contribution to American history this Society has devoted sixty-five years of consistent attention. The twenty-four volumes of the Monograph Series previously published range in their subject matter from New England, to Florida, to the Mid-West, to the Far West. We have tried to preserve for posterity the record of Catholic achievement. We value the Monograph Series especially because in it appear those scholarly studies which the publishing houses cannot sponsor for financial reasons and the scholarly quarterlies cannot publish because of length.

In this twenty-fifth volume we present to our members and to the public generally a masterly study by one of the ablest writers at work today in the field of American Catholic history. Father Peter Masten Dunne, of the Society of Jesus, has devoted his attention primarily to the Jesuit beginnings in Mexico. He is the author of *Pioneer Black Robes on the West Coast* (Berkeley, 1940), of *Pioneer Jesuits in Northern Mexico* (Berkeley, 1944), and of *Early Jesuit Missions in Tarahumara* (Berkeley, 1948). The present volume concerns the American activities of one of the ablest administrators and historians of the Jesuit order in Mexico in the years before the Franciscans took over their work. Andrés Pérez de Ribas was a man of great stature, and one to whom we owe much of our knowledge of these early beginnings of our Catholic culture in the New World. He has not before had a biographer. He has one now. The Society adds this volume to its list of Monographs with a sure knowledge of its intrinsic worth, and with great satisfaction at including on its list of authors the name of Peter Masten Dunne, S.J.

JOHN J. MENG

New York, March 15, 1951.

PREFACE

The writing of this biography of a great Spaniard and a great Westerner was suggested to me some years ago by Herbert Eugene Bolton of the University of California. The career of Andrés Pérez de Ribas illustrates in the missions the historic development of the frontier of New Spain north into what is now part of the territory of the United States. Although no Jesuit, not even Kino, penetrated into what is now the state of California, the Black Robes through their mission system built up the background and prepared the way for the later advance of the Franciscans two years after the suppression of the Spanish Jesuits which occurred in 1767. The position and activities of Ribas in Mexico after his retirement from the missions sheds light upon many a colorful detail of life in the great Capital hitherto unknown, and upon the triumphs and troubles of the Jesuits.

The author is grateful to Doctor Bolton, not only for suggesting the pleasant task of composing this little work, but also for his generosity in placing at my disposal the large collection of Jesuit source materials which are part of the Bolton Collection. May I here express my gratitude likewise to Father Pedro Leturia and to Father Edmond Lamalle of the central Jesuit archives for their forwarding of important materials; to Father Gerardo Decorme of Ysleta, Texas, for transcripts so kindly made by him of materials in the Jesuit archives of the ancient Province of New Spain; to Father W. Eugene Shiels for the use of photostatic documents taken from these same archives; and finally to Mrs. Richard Jones of Los Angeles for copying and re-copying the text.

PETER MASTEN DUNNE, S.J.
University of San Francisco
Feast of All Saints, 1950

ABBREVIATIONS USED IN NOTES

Archiv. S. J. Roman.—	*Archivum Societatis Jesu Romanum*
Archiv. Gen. Mis.—	*Archivo General, Misiones*
Archiv. Gen. Hist.—	*Archivo General, Historia*
A.G.I.	*Archivo General de Indias*
Archiv. Gral. MS., sin Fecha	*Archivo General Manuscrito, sin Fecha*
Alegre—	*Historia de la Compañía de Jesús en Nueva España*
Memorias—	*Memorias para la Historia de la Provincia de Sinaloa*
Ribas—	*Historia de los Triumphos de Nuestra Santa Fee*

NOTE: Ribas is cited according to book and chapter.

CONTENTS

CHAPTER I

Another Jesuit Comes to the New World

At Córdova on the Guadalquivir River in southern Spain in the year 1575 Andrés Pérez de Ribas entered the world. This baby, destined to fame, was born into the Europe of the Counter-Reformation, and he came upon a civilization torn with religious strife. It was four years after Lepanto and three since the massacre of St. Bartholomew. The Netherlands, under the rule of Spain and of King Philip II, were in revolt. The Duke of Alva, the man of blood and iron, had just been recalled from these provinces, and Antwerp had just been sacked by Spanish troops. In one year would come the Pacification of Ghent, which brought no peace.

Six years before the birth of Ribas the Catholics of the north of England had disastrously rebelled against the policy and persecutions of Queen Elizabeth, who had a few months later been excommunicated by Pope Pius V. In 1580 the Jesuits Campion and Parsons penetrated England in disguise to begin their historic missionary endeavor. In Germany the war of pens, spreading venom over reams of the written page, was to lead in four decades to the war of swords, in which the rivalries of religion and of royal houses were to begin the Thirty Years' War, which left Germany prostrate and set her back a hundred years.

Just beyond the borders of the Pyrenees in France the atrocious civil war, called the Wars of Religion, was to continue for over another decade, so weakening the kingdom that it almost slipped under the power of Spain. Italy was dominated politically by the latter, while at Rome Pope Gregory XIII was pursuing his vigorous policy for the furtherance of the militant Catholicism of the Counter-Reformation. The Company or Society of Jesus, the very soul of this reforming and renovating movement, had been founded by the Basque, Ignatius Loyola, thirty-five years before, and when Loyola's illustrious son Pérez de Ribas was born the great leader had been dead for nineteen years.

It was a troubled Europe, then, into which Andrés Pérez de Ribas came and yet Spain herself was not troubled. Owing to a rigorous policy of her kings and the strong Catholicism of her

1

people she had been able at the threshold of modern times to achieve and to maintain a national and religious unity which spared her the civil wars of France and of Germany but did not spare her persecution either political or religious. Jews and Moors were either persecuted or expelled to secure the unity of the Spanish peninsula.

However at the time of the birth of Andrés Pérez Spain was still young in her unity which matured under kings who became more absolute, but she was vigorous and powerful, holding the hegemony of Europe and ruling over Italy, Sicily, and the Low Countries, while the scions of her royal house were elected emperors of the German Empire. The Hapsburgs, indeed, bestrode Europe like a colossus, and while Philip II was reigning in Spain, Naples, Milan, and the Netherlands, his nephew Maximilian II was reigning over the traditional Hapsburg lands of which Austria was the nucleus and Hungary and Bohemia were recent additions. Maximilian was besides Emperor of Germany. He died the very year after Ribas was born, 1576, to be followed as Emperor by his son Rudolph II.

Philip II (1556-1598), founder of the Spanish branch of the Hapsburgs, besides ruling over his European kingdoms and provinces, possessed likewise his vast colonies of the Americas. It was thence he drew his revenue, gold and epecially silver from Mexico and Peru, which helped to make the sinews of his European wars;[1] it was thence he drew high prestige as the greatest monarch of the world which provoked the jealous enmity of England and of France. So great was the revenue brought to Spain from the New World that when the yearly galleons drew into Seville the price of silver on the market dropped appreciably.

Not only some of the best blood of Spain but large numbers of every manner of man were drawn from the Mother Country to America. Just casual reading will give an indication of this conclusion. A kinsman of Saint Teresa of Avila, Don Pedro Ruiz de Ahumada, became the wealthy patron of the novitiate church in Tepotzotlán.[2] The name of Loyola soon appeared in Peru

---

[1]Merriman, *The Rise of the Spanish Empire,* II, 207f.
[2]Valle, *El Convento de Tepotzotlán,* p. 16.

and again in Argentina. Don Martin Ignacio de Loyola, Bishop of Asunción in Paraguay in 1604, was a nephew of the saint.[3] Two of the earliest companions of Ignatius Loyola, Calixto Sá and Juan de Arteaga, had come to America.[4] In the course of a few decades after its discovery tens of thousands of Spaniards had migrated to the New World. When Nicolás de Ovando sailed to Santo Domingo in 1502 he brought with him twenty-five hundred colonists including many married couples.[5]

With this influx, of course, would be the missionary. With Columbus on his second voyage in 1493 came four priests representing three religious orders.[6] The Dominicans were established in Santo Domingo soon after its founding in 1495; Tecto, Ayora, and Gante, Franciscans, were in Mexico City four years after its conquest.[7] The Jesuits journeyed first to Brazil in 1549, only nine years after the Order's foundation. Three Jesuits came to Florida in 1566, while others followed later. Two years later a larger group arrived in Lima, Peru. After eight Jesuits were slain early in 1572 near the Chesapeake Bay, on the banks of the Rappahannock River, the stubborn soil of this province was abandoned and the Fathers went to Mexico City, fourteen of them, led by Pedro Sánchez, in the autumn of 1572. Their arrival had been prepared by Antonio Sedeño, one of the Florida group who had been residing in Havana.[8] Only three years, therefore, before Pérez de Ribas was born did the religious order he was destined to join set foot upon Mexican soil and begin that work of which Ribas was to become an important part in action, and an indispensable part in historiography.

During the time that Pérez de Ribas was developing into boyhood the work of the Jesuits in Mexico City and its environs grew and expanded. The Jesuits were not in Mexico four years when they had houses in Pátzcuaro, Guadalajara, Zacatecas and beautiful Oaxaca, these in addition to their college, San Pedro

---

[3]Charlevoix, The History of Paraguay, I, 232.
[4]Alegre, I, 43.
[5]Jones, An Introduction to Hispanic American History, p. 69.
[6]Bannon-Dunne, Latin America, p. 67.
[7]Priestley, The Mexican Nation: A History, p. 98, ed. 1930.
[8]Dunne, Pioneer Black Robes on the West Coast, p. 8.

y San Pablo, which had already been founded in the Capital.
Then the work expanded to Morelia, to Puebla, to Vera Cruz,
and finally out into the labors and the hazards of the permanent
missions among the savage.[9]

But so great was the need of the Jesuit missionary and so
ardent was the individual Jesuit to fill that need, that having
come west from Europe to Mexico as to a colony and a mission
field, the padres soon sped farther west across the wide Pacific
to found colleges and missions in the Philippine Islands. Indeed,
soon the Jesuits would have missionaries and martyrs on the
isolated Marianas, known today chiefly through their largest unit,
Guam.[10] Before the century was out reports began coming in
from the Philippines to Mexico City about the Jesuit colleges
founded at Manila and Zebu and concerning the missions on the
island of Tibogua and at Taybay, Butuang, Mindanao, and other
settlements in the wild.[11]

Very importantly, when Pérez de Ribas was a little boy of
only eight years, a certain Gonzalo de Tapia, countryman of Ribas,
sailed for the New World. He was not yet a priest, but was
soon to be ordained in Mexico City and immediately thereafter
to offer evidence of marked missionary qualities. In 1589 Gonzalo
de Tapia traveled from Mexico City far north with another Jesuit
on missionary work beyond Zacatecas to Durango, the capital of
a frontier province. The meeting he had at this time with the
Governor of the Province of Nueva Vizcaya, Don Rodrigo del
Río y Losa, a grizzled old soldier and frontiersman, settled his
future career. Tapia was sent in 1591 with Father Martín Pérez
to found a mission on the very rim of the frontier, a little place
on the Sinaloa River, San Felipe y Santiago, about fifty miles
inland from the Gulf of California.[12]

This was the beginning of the famous missions of the west coast

---

[9]Jacobsen, *Educational Foundations of the Jesuits in Sixteenth-Century
New Spain*, ch. V.

[10]Repetti, *History of the Society of Jesus in the Philippine Islands*,
part I.

[11]*Anua* of 1594, Archiv. S.J. Roman., Mex. 14, f. 121; *anua* of 1595,
Mexican copy.

[12]Shiels, *Gonzalo de Tapia*, ch. IX.

of North America, one of the greatest and perhaps the most successful of mission enterprises among savages in all colonial America, Paraguay excepted. Here is where Andrés Pérez de Ribas was to find his first great activity, but little did he know it then; when these missions were begun the lad was only fifteen years of age.

While Ribas was growing up into a youth and while he was beginning the studies which were to lead him to the priesthood, the mission in which he was eventually to begin his work was advancing with encouraging stride. Gonzalo de Tapia and Martín Pérez were laboring up and down the Sinaloa River and were baptizing their thousands of Indians. Then there came a setback. Tapia was murdered by one Nacabeba, rebel wizard or medicine-man. Things remained at a stand-still, but not for long. New missionaries came, the work began to spread, and by the beginning of the seventeenth century the Fuerte River in the modern Mexican state of Sinaloa was ready to receive the Black Robes. One of these would be Ribas himself.

While his mission field was being prepared for him in the wilds of western North America what were the activities of Pérez de Ribas in civilized Spanish Córdova? He had been receiving a secondary education and had finally advanced to university courses, for he had made up his mind to enter the priesthood. Since the time of San Fernando, that is, since King Ferdinand III in 1236 definitely took the city from the Moors, there has been up to the twentieth century an unbroken line of seventy-three bishops of Córdova, beginning with Lope de Fitero, consecrated about 1237. Late in the sixteenth century Bishop Mauricio Pazos y Figueroa built the Grand Seminary of San Pelagio. Whether Ribas made his ecclesiastical studies in the seminary of his native Córdova or whether he went for his higher studies to one of the great universities, Alcalá or Salamanca, we do not know.[13] But on one point we are certain: his training was of the best that Spain's *siglo de oro* could give and that meant as fine an education as was to be had anywhere in Europe. The excellence of

---

[13]Unfortunately there is no sketch in the sources of a life of Pérez de Ribas.

the training of this young cleric is evident, as we shall see, from a perusal of his writings. His breadth of vision and his style show him a humanist; his critical and scientific attitude show his higher education to have been well disciplined.

Perhaps Ribas took his earlier schooling with the Jesuits. As for Christian humanism, the Order was running the best educational establishments in Europe, especially in secondary education. Scholars and thinkers of the age, like Montaigne in France and Sir Edwin Sandys, John Selden, and Francis Bacon in England, were well aware of this excellence, which led Bacon to his well-known encomium of Jesuit efficiency in education: "The noblest part of the ancient discipline has been restored in the Jesuit colleges. When I consider their industry and skill both in cultivating learning and in forming character I cannot help saying: *talis cum sis, utinam noster esses.*"[14] By the express approval of Ignatius Loyola himself there had been opened at the end of 1553 a Jesuit college in Córdova which, both in writing and in drama, attracted the attention of the town.[15] It is quite probable that Ribas received his earlier education here, and here is where he may first have come to know and to admire the individuals of that Order he was later to join.

His vocation to the religious life apparently developed late, unless there had been some obstacle which prevented his becoming a religious earlier, for he did not enter the Society of Jesus until 1602, his twenty-seventh year and after he had already been ordained a priest. He had already gone through three years of philosophy, in which he had received the licentiate, and four of theology.[16]

It is remarkable about Andrés Pérez that no sooner had he been admitted as a novice into the Company than he was shipped post-haste over to the Americas. And we may be sure he did not travel alone. The Jesuits always crossed the Atlantic in groups. Father Pedro Sánchez was the head of fourteen, leading

---

[14]"Since such you are, would that you were ours." Quoted in Simpson's *Edmund Campion, Jesuit Protomartyr of England,* p. 520. Bacon was a Protestant which explains this expression of his desire.

[15]Farrell, *The Jesuit Code of Liberal Education,* p. 112.

[16]*Archiv. S.J. Roman., Mex.* 4, f. 153.

in 1572 the first band to Mexico.[17] Twenty-three came over together in 1584 and among them was Gonzalo de Tapia.[18] The
journey would take Andrés Pérez close to three months if all
went well. He may not have fared so finely as Father Juan
María Ratkay who made the same journey eighty years later
in company of the new Bishop of Manila, dining in the captain's
room and having his meals topped off with candy or preserves.[19]
But he would perform each day some spiritual exercises. For all
the passengers there would be Mass early each morning or at
least morning prayer, and Ribas as a Jesuit had the spiritual
exercise of his morning meditation to perform and as a novice a
shorter meditation in the evening. Breakfast may have been at
nine and dinner at four, as with Father Ratkay, and the day
would end with the singing of the litany of the Virgin Mary and
the Salve Regina. Beginning with Francis Xavier in 1541 the
Jesuit while traveling at sea was accustomed to engage in apostolic work among the passengers and the crew. Xavier enhanced
the Christian spirit of the sailors of his craft; Ratkay succeeded
in persuading all the passengers of his ship to receive the sacraments of confession and Holy Communion. Ribas, though a
Jesuit novice, was also a priest and probably did his share of con-
structive spiritual influence.

By the time that Ribas crossed the Atlantic in 1602 hundreds
of Spanish and Portuguese Jesuits had done the same. Not all
went to Mexico. Groups of Portuguese continued south to
Brazil, while many Spaniards entering New Spain proceeded
across the Pacific to the Philippines. Large numbers had already
gone to Peru. Those destined for the province of New Spain
would sail south of the Greater Antilles, slide by the northern
coast of Yucatán into the Gulf of Mexico and disembark at the
fort of San Juan de Ulua and the port of Vera Cruz. Thence the
road wound west over the old historic route of Cortés. Ribas and
his group of Jesuits would leave the unwholesome tropics of the
coast through salubrious Jalapa, past Orizaba, towering its graceful cone of snow to the skies, along the high plateau into Puebla.

[17]Alegre, I, 50.
[18]Shiels, *op. cit.*, p. 49.
[19]Bolton, *Rim of Christendom*, p. 66.

After a rest the party would continue west, passing very close to the two great peaks, Iztaccihuatl and Popocatepetl, shrouded in their shawl of snow and keeping perpetual watch over the ancient plateau of Anáhuac, Valley of Waters, where the capital city is set like a gem. A more southerly route often taken was just as picturesque. The Europeans must have marveled.

But Ribas did not continue with his group nor did he at this time enter the valley. The fair city of Puebla de los Angeles was to be his home for the two years which ensued and here he was to complete his novitiate. The novitiate proper was at Tepotzotlán thirty miles north northwest of Mexico City, but it was not exceptional that smaller groups or even one should make his two years of probation elsewhere. As a matter of fact the Jesuit annual letters inform us that there was a novitiate in Puebla in 1602.[20] Here then was Ribas' home during 1603 and most of 1604 and here it was that he went through that intensive cultivation of the spiritual life and of supernatural asceticism which is the characteristic feature of religious novitiate.[21] Excellent training it was for the future missionary and, indeed, a proximate preparation for the work, for when his two years were finished he went directly to the missions.

Well prepared was he in 1604 for the arduous labors and peculiar hazards of a missionary among the savage. Amid the strict discipline and severe asceticism of the two years of his novitiate Ribas had gone through the Spiritual Exercises of his leader, St. Ignatius Loyola. These exercises, athletics of the spirit, consisted of a month of silence spent in meditation on the fundamental truths of philosophy and religion and in consideration of the purposes and ideals of the Christian founder, Jesus Christ. The exercises include self-examination—scrutiny of weaknesses of the mind and soul—and efforts to eliminate defects; they embody strong encouragement and high inspiration looking forward to the possession of God and towards a courageous embracing of the difficult career of priest, missionary, and apostle.

20*Archiv. S.J. Roman., Mex.* 14, f. 276.
21*Archiv. S.J. Roman, Mex.* 8, f. 266f. and *Mex.* 4, f. 153.

Now finally in 1604, three years before the first English settlement at Jamestown, Ribas would pass on west from Puebla, through the divide which threaded close to the two white sentinels, then down into the valley of waters, Anáhuac, and into the first city of North America, Mexico, metropolis of the New World. Metropolis indeed it was even at this early date with its viceregal court, its archbishop, its tribunals of justice, its nobility, its university, its colleges, its cathedral, its churches and convents; with its eight thousand Spaniards, thirty thousand dwellings, and, including Indians, possibly one hundred thousand inhabitants in all.[22] Suburbs close at hand augmented the size and importance of the capital of Mexico.

But Andrés Pérez did not tarry long in the capital. The missions called him north, his vow of obedience was put to a test not difficult for him. By the fall of that very year of 1604 he was far north at San Felipe on the Río Sinaloa, a stream which drops down from the Sierra Madre Occidental and throws its waters into the southern reaches of the Gulf of California.

---

[22]Priestley, *op. cit.*, p. 140.

CHAPTER II

EDGE OF THE FRONTIER

Andrés Pérez de Ribas, then, came to the missions of the West Coast in 1604. The circumstances were these. The great captain, Diego Martínez de Hurdaide, had opened up the country of the Río Fuerte by the defeat of the treacherous Suaqui Indians and of the warlike Sinaloa tribe. The Jesuit Black Robes could now advance to this river and begin to evangelize the natives who lived upon its banks, including the mild Ahomes down near the sea. But it was impossible to begin this new venture for lack of men. Gonzalo de Tapia had been murdered in 1594; Hernando de Santarén had been called away to the mountainous mission of Topia in 1598; Father Alonzo had but looked at the country, got sick, and returned south. Thus there were remaining only four priests, Pérez, Velasco, Méndez, and Villafañe, to attend the missions on the Sinaloa. They were aided by the efficient Jesuit brother, Francisco de Castro. If the missions were to advance to the Fuerte more men were needed. Captain Hurdaide, whose head and arm and heart were taken up wholly with the advancement of the missions, determined to go to Mexico to fetch the padres. And he succeeded. He came back with two, Andrés Pérez de Ribas and Cristóbal de Villalta.

The journey north and west from Mexico City was at first uneventful; later savagery asserted itself. Captain Hurdaide had invited some Indian chiefs to accompany him on the journey south, that they might behold the splendors of the capital and be recipients of the courtesy of the Viceroy and the kindness of the fathers. Returning thus entertained and consoled to their country the Indian chiefs would spread over all the tribes the high prestige of the Christian religion and of the King of Spain. Some of these caciques were from the Sinaloa River; others were friendly pagans from the Fuerte who lived near the Suaquis and were called Tehuecos from their pueblo of Tehueco on the banks of the river. A stroke of good diplomacy this, to take these chiefs to the capital.

It was four of these, however, who created the incident of the return journey and they were all from Tehueco. The party, consisting of Captain Hurdaide, the two padres, some soldiers, the

10

chiefs, the pack-mules, with the muleteers, had trudged three hundred and fifty miles along valley and upland on that great and high plateau of central Mexico. Their destination was San Felipe, over four hundred miles farther northwest. They had already reached Zacatecas, pioneer mining town, when it was found one morning that four of the Tehueco caciques were missing. They had stolen away secretly in the night and made off to their own country. The instinct of a savage led them unerringly. Turning west they traversed the great mountain range called the Sierra Madre and on the coast near Culiacán they slew three Indians to get their mounts. They sped to Tehueco, carrying the heads of the three they had slain, spread disquieting reports, and then fled into the mountains to their friends the Tepahues.[1]

Naturally the desertion of the chiefs disturbed the travelers. Hurdaide made after the fugitives for he knew the harm they might do in the spread of evil report. But pursuit was vain and there was nothing for it but to speed up the rest of the journey in order that trouble at home might be prevented or put down by the early appearance of Captain Hurdaide himself. The party went north beyond Durango, then struck west across the Sierra Madre at Topia, and thence down into the long, narrow plain of the west coast to Culiacán, which lay just across the gulf from the tip of Lower California. A hundred miles north along comparatively easy country brought the travelers to San Felipe after a trek of more than eight hundred miles.

Ribas had never before made so long a journey on land; never before had he beheld such expanse of sweeping plain or traversed the chasmed ruggedness of so great a cordillera. Tired he doubtless was, for the going had been in haste from Zacatecas on. But the welcome given at San Felipe by Father Martín Pérez, superior of the mission, was warm and benevolently fraternal. The Spanish Jesuit even to this day receives affectionately his brother from afar, and seldom, if ever, within the Order, is a Jesuit a stranger in a strange house. Besides, Ribas and Villalta were the long-awaited recruits which would make it possible now for the frontiers of

---

[1] Ribas, II, 29.

Christianity and of Spain to push on another sixty miles and stabilize themselves on the banks of the Río Fuerte.[2]

San Felipe, the present Sinaloa, rested on the slope of a lone hill which rises from the edge of the Río Sinaloa, then often called the Río de San Felipe. From the brow of this hill Ribas could regale his eyes with the prospect of a magnificent panorama. East rose the long blue line of the Sierra Madre; west he looked out over the plain some sixty miles to the sea. West and a little north were the reaches of the lower Fuerte River, where would lie the fair fields of his first missionary labors. A thrust of hills running across the lower levels hid the banks of the Fuerte from his view. But he could see a pass through these hills, gateway to the Suaquis. Lower down and near the sea were the mild Ahomes. Farther west islands which fringe the shore rose like ghosts in lavender out of a shimmering sea.

It was late in 1604 when the two new missionaries arrived near the scene of their future labors. As soon as word sped over hill and dale that the long-awaited padres were come delegations from the tribes of the Fuerte arrived to beg that the missionaries be immediately sent to them. This would be a frequent and touching recurrence on this west coast. The Ahomes, the Suaquis, the Tehuecos, and the Sinaloas, all put in their petition. The Ahomes had always been friendly to Hurdaide and the Spaniards; long ago they had asked that missionaries might come to them. Indeed, it was to protect the Ahomes from the assaults of their enemies, the Suaquis, that Hurdaide had set out in 1602 finally to subdue the country.[3]

Already in 1601 the Captain by a ruthless action had smashed the pride of the Suaquis in slaying through a clever ruse forty-two of their caciques.[4] Two years later the whole country was subdued by the submission of both the Suaquis and the Sinaloas. The fathers, thereafter, had some contact with these tribes; one or another savage had already been the recipient of baptism. They had learned to fear and to respect, even to love, the Spaniard,

---

[2]Ribas, II, 29; Alegre, I, 426.
[3]Ribas, II, 27; anua of 1602, Memorias, pp. 400ff.
[4]Ribas, II, 21-22.

represented by the strong arm of Captain Hurdaide and by
the affable manner of the gentle missionary. With this background of understanding it becomes less astounding, but remains
consolingly surprising, that these natives of the Fuerte, formerly
treacherous and warlike, should now send delegations asking that
Ribas and his fellow missionary come to live among them. From
the Suaquis on this occasion came the chief Venturo, whose life
had been spared through the intercession of the interpreter Luisa
(a friendly Suaqui) at the time of Hurdaide's first conquest.
Luisa also came. From the Tehuecos came Lanzarote, already a
Christian, with his wife and some other caciques. The Sinaloas
sent their leaders as did the Ahomes.[5]

The padres, however, could not depart immediately for the new
and fertile fields. The year 1604 had been difficult. A great flood,
caused by the overflow of the Sinaloa and its tributaries, ruined
three mission churches on the lower river, whose construction
Father Hernando de Villafañe had directed with joy and pride.[6]
Pedro Méndez had to perch with his neophytes in trees until
the waters subsided.[7] Famine and hunger followed, which gave
opportunity to the medicine-man to scoff at the God of the Christians and led certain pueblos of neophytes to rebel and disperse
to the hills.[8] Sixteen hundred and four was therefore a troubled
year, and Pérez de Ribas could not yet inaugurate his missionary
labors.

For another thing, the new missionaries could not take up
their residence among the Indians until they knew the language.
In the multiform and endless divisions of the uncivilized state
of the natives, the idiom might differ with every river and sometimes with every few miles. Father Juan Bautista de Velasco was
engaged in writing a grammar of the language spoken on the
Sinaloa River.[9] These Indians belonged for the most part to the
Cáhita nation, but they did not extend all along the river. The
Cáhitas were broken into by the Nios and the Ocoronis, and down

---

[5]Ribas, III, 2.
[6]*Anua* of 1604, *Memorias,* pp. 408f.
[7]Ribas, II, 25; *Memorias, loc. cit.*
[8]*Anua* of 1605, *Archiv. S.J. Roman.,* f. 429.
[9]*Anua* of 1604, *Memorias,* p. 412.

by the sea a different nation, called the Guasaves, spoke a different language. It was the same on Río Fuerte. Down by the sea the Guasave tongue was general but not universal. Up the river the Cáhita speech was used among the Suaquis, Tehuecos, and Sinaloas, while farther upstream near and into the fringes of the Sierra Madre lived the Chínipas, Huites, Témoris, Zoes, and Tubares. Each of these last mentioned probably spoke the same dialect except the Huites.[10] Pérez de Ribas could not go immediately, therefore, up to the Fuerte River. The language of his savages must first be mastered. And he must learn two languages for he would be given the lower river and work among the Ahomes, who were of the Guasave tribe, and among the Suaquis, who were of the Cáhita.

A certain measure of caution likewise had to be observed. The Mexican savage was proverbially fickle, often treacherous. And although the country of the Fuerte had been subdued and its inhabitants had become apparently friendly, Hurdaide, the military captain, and Martín Pérez, the Jesuit superior, realized full well it would not do prematurely to plant missionaries singly and permanently among the savages of the Fuerte. It would be some two years before three missionaries would go up to make their residence in different sections of the northern river. In the meantime the savages did their best to impress both the fathers and the Captain with their good will. And they performed here a touching gesture of faith and confidence, which was later and elsewhere on the coast often to be repeated: they brought their sons down to the Sinaloa River and left them under the charge of fathers at San Felipe to be trained and instructed in the Faith. When the missionaries would finally go into their country these boys would be an aid in the general instruction which must take place before the baptism of the adults.[11]

The savages did more. They got into conference with Hurdaide and the fathers to talk over ways and means of organizing the future evangelization of their tribes. They were willing to gather

---

[10]Cf. Sauer, *The Distribution of Aboriginal Tribes and Languages in Northwestern Mexico,* pp. 23ff. and 32ff.

[11]Ribas, III, 2.

themselves more closely into pueblos in districts suitable for the building of a church. Formerly they had been accustomed to live in a rather dispersed fashion on ground where they had their plantings of corn and of cotton. It was decided that they would build their huts, called *jacales,* clustered around the spot where the future churches would rise, and these latter would be great structures for so wild a country, built of adobe and large timbers. The chiefs too would in the meantime prepare their people for the coming of the missionaries and they further agreed to send messengers and ambassadors to neighboring tribes to bring to them the good news of the coming of Christianity.[12]

Thus were matters all arranged for the beginning of the missionary labors of Father Andrés Pérez de Ribas. These labors were destined to be great and fruitful. They would advance the frontier far up the coast of the Gulf of California and bring it ultimately, not long after Ribas' death, close to the gates of Alta California.

---

[12]Ribas, III, 2.

CHAPTER III

Introduction To The Savage

All these things being arranged, affairs worked out perfectly. Nor is this statement an exaggeration, unless the eye-witness, Pérez de Ribas himself, and the official reports mantle over the shadows and unduly admit the sunshine. Since elsewhere our sources expose the shadows too, we would expect them to do it here likewise did the shadows exist. But the sunshine of the original narratives of more than three hundred years ago reflect the sunshine which today actually warms and engoldens these fertile coasts.

The superior, Martín Pérez, began to realize that the two fresh missionaries, Ribas and Villalta, would not suffice for the whole district of the Fuerte River. He therefore decided to add a third for the *entrada,* or entrance, north. Father Pérez would sacrifice Pedro Méndez from Río Sinaloa that Río Fuerte might prosper the more. The choice was intelligent, for Méndez had been now ten years in the mission, arriving with Father Velasco in August, 1594, the very week of Tapia's murder. Méndez had had various experiences up and down the Sinaloa and its tributary, the Ocoroni. He had evangelized Indians on both river banks; he had organized a school for Indian boys; he had attended his dying neophytes when they were laid low by the plague. To him was assigned the middle reaches of the Fuerte. Upstream among the surly Sinaloas Cristóbal de Villalta was sent, while to Pérez de Ribas the lower levels of the stream were assigned, the Suaquis and the mild Ahomes. Ribas would first go to the Ahomes, and from there he would visit their neighbors, the Suaquis, farther up the river.

There was wisdom in this choice, for the Ahomes were already well attuned to the spirit of the Christian religion. They had from the start been more friendly and never inimical to the Spaniard. They had been the first to put in a request for a padre. They were of a more developed culture than their neighbors a few miles down the coast. "They live in pueblos, wear clothing, and plant crops. Their land is very fertile."[1] Among these Ahomes, moreover,

---

[1] *Anua* of 1605, *Archiv. S.J. Roman., Mex.* 14, f. 431.

16

there had been living a Christian who was blind, one of the ten thousand odd who by this time had been gathered into the fold in the country of the Sinaloa. This blind neophyte at their own request began to teach the Ahomes the foundations of the Christian religion. True to the promise they had made when Pérez de Ribas first came into the country they had built a church or chapel, set up a cross before it, and repaired thither twice daily to go over and to memorize the truths of religion which their blind mentor had taught them. Their enthusiasm was so great that they set about building another and larger church modeled on the one they had seen at San Felipe.[2]

Fortunate indeed was Ribas to go among savages so mild, so willing, and so well prepared. His first visit to them was made in 1605. His coming had been announced and he was overjoyed at the reception which was tendered him. The blind Christian had been a wonderful leaven among the Ahomes, for what awaited Ribas equalled or surpassed anything he could have dreamed of.

The Ahome pueblo consisted of between three hundred and four hundred families. When word came that Ribas was approaching, the Indians came out joyously in procession to meet him, led by their chief on horseback. Their persons were decorated in all their savage finery, with feathers, skins of animals, and ornaments of shell. Each carried in his hand fresh-cut boughs, while in front of the group a large cross adorned with foliage and the gay plumage of birds was borne high like a banner. As the Ahomes advanced towards Ribas they chanted the Christian doctrine and the divine praises. Arbors made of foliage were placed along the way.[3]

So impressed was Ribas that he tells us it reminded him of the entry of Christ into Jerusalem on the Sunday of the palms.

Ribas was now escorted to an arbor erected for the occasion. Hundreds of the tribe were gathered about this shelter. There were mothers with their babies and that first day three hundred infants received the sacrament of baptism, while the Christian names given to each were entered into a book.[4]

---

[2]*Anua* of 1605, *loc. cit.*, f. 432.
[3]Ribas, III, 4.
[4]*Anua* of 1605, *loc. cit.*; Ribas, III, 2.

That night there was great rejoicing. The parents of the baptized were hosts to the Indian godfathers and godmothers, come for the occasion from Sinaloa, whom they regaled with tortillas and tamales. Bonfires were lit and speech-making was prolonged far into the night. Eight days Ribas tarried here on this the beginning of his activities on the river. He learned much of Ahome habits of which he wrote later. He experienced most consolingly the happiness and satisfaction of this people in having their father at last among them. He made arrangements for the baptism of the adults which would take place on his next visit and he instructed that they prepare to build a larger church. The Ahomes pointed out to Ribas the passes through which their former enemies, the Suaquis, were accustomed to enter their lands to harass their pueblo and to annoy their women. Hurdaide had put a stop to that.[5]

Here began a most touching friendship of the Jesuit Andrés Pérez de Ribas with these Ahomes of the Guasave nation on the lower Fuerte near the coast of the Gulf of California. The missionary says in a passage quoted elsewhere:[6] "The natural goodness, gentleness, and fidelity of this people . . . can be described in a thought which I have often had. During most dangerous times when all the tribes of the province were threatening to rise, the one refuge that was offered me until the tempest passed was to go, even into the mountains, with my faithful Ahomes. With them would I find greater security than with any other tribe of the province, so great was their love and respect for their spiritual father. And during the eleven years that I lived among them and instructed them, never once did I witness any movement of disquietude or of inconstancy." It was quite evident that these Ahomes were the special favorites of Ribas among all the tribes that he was to live with. He describes their dress, their food, their manner of hunting and fishing; he praises their virtues, especially their chastity, speaks of the absence of witches and wizards (the notorious *hechicero* pest of the missionaries), and of the custom of wailing and moaning over the dead which lasted for months. This

---

[5]Ribas, III, 2.
[6]Dunne, *Pioneer Black Robes on the West Coast*, p. 85.

last the missionary had to eradicate, because of its superstition and (as we guess) because it jangled his nerves and kept him awake at nights.[7]

These details are refreshing. Seldom do we have them from the pen of the missionary himself, but in the case of Ribas we are fortunate for he was both missionary and historian. Rarely if ever in the annals of the missions of all the world can we find such charming narratives and such attractive pictures as are given us in the pages of the great work of Pérez de Ribas, and well did he name it *The Triumphs of the Faith*. From the ease, the charm, and the success of his first work among the Ahomes we can understand his enthusiasm and we can glimpse his inner peace. Ribas was fortunate and he knew it; we are fortunate that he knew it and wrote it.

----

[7]Ribas, III, 3. For fuller details cf. Dunne, *op. cit.,* ch. IX.

CHAPTER IV

The Treacherous Suaquis Are Tamed

After this joyous entrada to the Ahomes Ribas prepared to make another to the Suaquis. Both tribes had been given him for his own. After eight days, therefore, he left for upriver to be introduced to his more savage children whose record, so contrary to that of the Ahomes, had been writ in blood and war.

The traveler today may pass along the route which Ribas took upstream from the Ahome land to the Suaquis. A road, rough and of infinite dust, leaves Ahome and passes hard by all the mission sites which sit upon the stream. From Ahome near the sea to Vaca close against the tall sierras was set by the early padres a line of missions shining like jewels upon the river's silver thread: Ahome, San Miguel, Mochicahue, Charay, Sivirijoa, Tehueco, Toro, Vaca—these were the missions of the Fuerte begun in 1605 by Ribas, Méndez, and Villalta. In each particular site, except possibly at Ahome, the ruins of these pioneer missions still exist drooping down upon the landscape like flowers without water. At Ahome it is doubtful whether the old adobes which are left date back to the time of Ribas; Tehueco is almost not a ruin, so firm yet stand its walls. The file of time has worn down the church of Sivirijoa almost to the ground, while Vaca, still fairly well preserved and standing on the banks of the growling river as it issues from the sierra, attests the importance of the mission which Villalta founded long ago among the Sinaloas.

San Miguel and Mochicahue are among the pueblos which lay in the country of the Suaquis. The former was built after Ribas left the river; but Mochicahue is rich in lore in the pages of our missionary author. It exhibits today the least picturesque of the ruins. They consist merely of a block of adobes jutting out in the rear from an abandoned and unfinished structure in brick. The mission San Miguel lower down the stream and very close to Ahome country presents a more picturesque ruin. The whole rectangular outline of the ancient structure is marked by at least a few layers of old adobes; those which formed the higher section of the wall have been worn to powder by wind and rain and lie in a shapeless pile upon the ground like the talus of a cliff. In other parts of the ruin the walls rise high, almost to where the roof has been. Here in 1934 on a January morning early in the month, when the sun had just risen in a clear sky, had gathered a hundred of these Suaqui Indians, men and women, to commemorate without benefit of clergy the Feast of the Epiphany, the meaning of which Pérez de Ribas had taught their ancestors over three centuries before.[1]

Ribas then came to the Suaquis probably direct from the Ahomes. They were expecting him and there came to meet him and to escort him in honor to their chief pueblo of Mochicahue the interpreter and old friend of the Spaniards, the Christian Luisa; there came Venturo, the cacique who had been spared from hanging at the intercession of Luisa with Hurdaide, and there came other magnates of the Suaqui tribe. Ribas tells us that they gave him a joyous and hearty welcome, though we miss the details whose narration made so colorful his entrance to the Ahomes. The Suaquis came forth without their bows and arrows, a sign of utter friendliness and trust, and they led him to an arbor made of branches, an *enramada,* which was to be his temporary dwelling. Another such fabric was to serve as a chapel.

The savages gave Ribas every sign of respect. They kissed his hand, while some took his hand and placed it on their head. They gathered all about the enramada and the principal caciques welcomed him. Ribas made them a speech explaining to them the purpose of his coming. He said in part: "I come not for war, because I carry no arms, nor am I with soldiers. But I come to assist you and to be your father and to teach you the way of salvation."[2] Well could Ribas say this and well could it be appreciated by the savages. They had seldom if ever before seen the Spaniard in their country unaccompanied by a guard of soldiers and at this very time Hurdaide was unwilling to entrust Méndez to the tender mercies of the Tehuecos, or Villalta to the Sinaloas, without an escort of arms. The missionary concluded his speech with the exhortation that no time should be lost in their acceptance of Christianity which would bring them under the protection of

---

[1]Dunne, *Pioneer Black Robes on the West Coast,* ch. IX and illustrations.
[2]Ribas, III, 11.

God and of the King of Spain. As in the other missions of the Sinaloa River, the best way to make a start, said Ribas, was with the baptism of the children. The chiefs consented and the mothers were willing.

Ribas bent himself immediately to his holy work. Interpreter Luisa knew well the procedure and was an indispensable assistant. She had the mothers bring up their babies and their other children who were young enough for baptism without instruction. They came timidly forward with their offspring; some were babes in arms, others toddling youngsters. They were arranged in order so that Ribas might pass expeditiously from one to another pouring on the head of each the saving waters. Three hundred children were that first day made Christians, and Luisa was probably the universal godmother.

After this first day's fruitful labor Ribas passed on to two other pueblos, which he does not name, but one of which may have been Charay. In each of these the same procedure took place so that at the end of a few days eight hundred had been baptized. Those who were far off in the fields he sent for, that they too might come with their children to receive the sacrament.

But there were old people about too. Some Ribas learned were close to a hundred years of age. These he considered should be treated as children, for though the adults should not be baptized without instruction in the Faith, these very ancient people were in danger of early or sudden death. It was advisable Ribas thought, to confer upon them the sacrament without further delay. Thus twenty-seven of these aged were admitted to the Faith. Ribas was conscientious enough to favor these immediately with full instruction and therefore during these days that he tarried among the Suaquis he devoted two instructions a day to the old so that, should death intervene, they would be ready to part the curtains to the other life. For this purpose too he blessed the marriages of those who had a living mate, so that to one sacrament was added another. These twenty-seven old people were thus given preference; the others would need longer training and a more general course of instruction.[3]

---

[3]*Ibid.*

Before leaving the Suaquis Ribas was able to bring about a more practical organization of the tribe, better fitted for the instruction and baptism of the adults which would take place later. He prevailed upon them to abandon one of their three pueblos and to concentrate their population into two. The Black Robe had opportunity during these days to ask the Suaquis, formerly so fierce and treacherous, now so gentle and docile, what it was that kept them so long a time in a state of enmity towards the Spaniards and the padres. They replied they had been deceived by their medicine-men, their hechiceros, who constantly spoke ill of the white man. But now, said they, it was certain they were mistaken and they were very happy to receive the faith of the Spaniards. Ribas on his part exerted himself to preserve these excellent dispositions among them.[4]

In November, 1606, a sort of formal entrada was made by Captain Hurdaide, probably for the good psychological purpose of impressing the different tribes of the Fuerte and introducing to the four groups of that river the three missionaries who were working along its banks. From Ahome upstream along the course of the Fuerte Captain Hurdaide with the three fathers and thirty-nine soldiers made his way. The company was greeted by the natives and as they went from pueblo to pueblo children were presented for baptism.[5] Thus were Ribas, Méndez and Villalta presented formally to the Ahomes, the Suaquis, the Tehuecos, and the Sinaloas. They returned to San Felipe before taking up definite and permanent residence on Río Fuerte. It was only now, probably, at the end of 1606, that Ribas resided permanently among his people.

---

[4]*Ibid.*
[5]*Anua* of 1606, *Archiv. S.J. Roman., Mex.* 14, f. 488.

CHAPTER V

RIBAS DOWN NEAR THE SEA

We do not know how long Ribas remained among the Suaquis. He does not tell us, nor does anybody else. The only thing we find is this: "Returning within a short time to revisit the new flock I found the Ahomes very happy and, since they had already gathered the materials, waiting to start the building of their church."[1] His visit to the Suaquis may have been for two weeks, it may have been a month. In any case, he shortly returned to his first and always strongest love, the Ahomes. Again he was encouraged, again delighted. They gave him a warm and joyous welcome. He found that in his absence these Ahomes had assembled materials for the church he had instructed them to build, and they pressed him for the baptism not only of the infants whom he could not reach during his first visit and of those born since, but for the baptism even of all the adults.

He set to work immediately. He completed the baptism of the infants of the tribe to the number of five hundred and superintended and organized the building of the church. It was Chartres in France all over again on a small scale. Men and women bent their energies to the task of rearing what was to them a monster edifice. They made the adobes, fashioned the timbers, and gathered and arranged the straw for the roof. Ribas, as smartly diplomatic as he was self-sacrificing, lent a hand to the labor. The adobes rose tier upon tier to form the four walls of the structure; then the great beams were stretched across from wall to wall; a matted plaiting of osiers was laid over them; and finally the roof was completed with straw overlain with mud. The Ahomes were proud of what they had constructed. Though rough and poor, their church seemed to them a grand edifice. Never before had anything like it been seen among them. Like the cathedrals of Europe in the Middle Ages, this church would be for the Ahomes the center of their spiritual and cultural life.

It is evident Ribas tarried long among the Ahomes this time, for the church was not built in a few days, or even weeks.[2]

---

[1] Ribas, III, 5.

[2] *Anua* of 1606, *Archiv. S.J. Roman., Mex.* 14, f. 488.

He had leisure on this occasion to instruct and to baptize the adults. The old cacique and his son were the most important of the neophytes to receive the saving waters and all the tribe followed suit. Their pagan names were changed to Christian: Nobfoot, Hawk-eye, and Spindle-hair were changed to Michael, John, and Peter. A pagan, murderer of Tapia on the Sinaloa, was called Nacabeba which meant Struck-on-the-Ear. The Yaquis were named from feats of bravery they had performed; for instance, a Yaqui would be called Ten-men-killed, Three-men-killed, Killed-a-man-on-the-mountain, -near-the-river, -in-the-field.[3]

The Ahomes, says Ribas, were sometimes, but not as often as the Yaquis or other tribes, named from the people they had killed. But now, Christianity of the spirit must soften down this barbarism of the flesh. And so the old cacique was named Don Pedro after the Rock upon which the Church was built, and his son, sonorously, Don Miguel. The name of the Archangel Michael suited the latter, says our pious chronicler, for like Michael of the heavenly hosts, the earthly Don Miguel exercised the office of guide for his people. Captain Hurdaide, as diplomatic as he was efficient, and well in harmony with the missionary, appointed Don Miguel governor of all that district on the lower river, the chief representing thus the jurisdiction of Spain over this now subject people. The appointment was a great honor, for this son of the old cacique was given a sword and Spanish dress, with boots, doublet, feathered hat, and the rest of it. Thus encouraged Don Miguel aided well the missionary. He made a list of all the families in order that none might miss instruction for baptism, and every morning he went to the church to aid in the instruction of those who came. Thus were all the tribe of the Ahomes brought into the Faith.[4]

So happy were these people over all that had come to them that they asked Ribas if they might celebrate their new-found faith by a dance. He was broad and human enough to consent. It would be done in the Christian and not in the pagan spirit. Drinking would not be allowed and chaste manners would prevail through-

---

[3]Ribas, V, 1.
[4]Ribas, III, 5.

out. So was it done and the Ahomes were happy under the care of their missionary.[5]

Auspiciously then did Andrés Pérez de Ribas begin his eleven years' residence on the lower Fuerte. It will be recalled that when the four tribes of the Fuerte sent delegates to San Felipe in 1604 to beg that the new missionaries be sent to them, it was part of the stipulation that they get in touch with the neighboring tribes and announce to them the glad tidings. Now down the river from the Ahomes near the sea and scattered over and along the dunes and estuaries of the coast were other tribes of the Guasave nation, kith and kin to the Ahomes. These were the Batucaris, the Bacorigues, and the Comoporis.

The savage is curious. Word concerning what was going on at Ahome sped over the hillocks near the sea and over the flats and levels of the coast. Caciques from these people came in to the pueblo to see for themselves. The padre received them well, with all the charm of his cultivated Latin nature. He gave them gifts: colored glass beads, a needle, a knife, and a horseshoe they could play with or sharpen for a *macana*. These savage visitors went back to their people and spread the good word which traveled far along those coasts. These shaggy and isolated peoples heard of friends now and of a charming and kindly Black Robe. No longer did they hear of enemies. Sympathetic contacts had thus been made which in time would yield their fruit.

Many months had not passed when a portion of the Batucaris, living on some low-lying hills off to the southeast, came in a body to the pueblo of Ahome not for a passing visit, but for a permanent residence. They wanted to enjoy the blessings of their kinsmen, persuaded to this step by the diplomacy of Ribas and his neophyte Don Miguel. They set up their huts on a fringe of the Ahome pueblo and kept their own government under their own cacique. Being very close to hand now the Batucaris could be instructed and baptized.[6]

There was another group of these Batucaris living nearer the coast, a ragged people, nomadic in their habits, who supported

---

[5]*Ibid.*
[6]Ribas, III, 6.

themselves by the fruits of the chase. They were not very particular, however, as to their diet; for when they could not shoot the deer or snare the rabbit, they would be satisfied with moles and rats, gophers and snakes. This group could not be coaxed to settle down at Ahome. But Ribas did persuade them to clear some level ground near where they roamed and to choose it as the site for their own pueblo. After slow and patient working with these rags of humanity Ribas succeeded in persuading some to settle here under a cacique. Gradually he got them to build a little chapel; finally he was able to baptize their children to the number of about a hundred.[7]

The Bacorigues were of a somewhat higher type. A number of them were quite willing to come to live on a "beautiful and cool level" which Ribas had selected as a good site for a pueblo. They cleared the ground and set up their huts. Only a few came at first, but others followed, including their cacique, a giant fellow who had the reputation among them of being able single-handed to slay a crocodile. The blind Christian, who had done so much to prepare the Ahomes before Ribas' residence among them, was sent down to the Bacorigues as catechist. Soon they were ready for the work of Ribas. He came and baptized two hundred of their children.[8]

The conversion of the Comoporis is an intriguing story. It offers, moreover, a typical example of the gentle arts these early Black Robes used to catch the savage in Peter's net. What Ribas was doing down along the coast Villalta was pursuing in among the tall sierras. The Comoporis were "as fierce and brave a tribe as lived in Sinaloa, so that even the Suaquis feared them. Never had these tribes met in conflict but that the Suaquis had left some comrades dead upon the field." As often in human contacts one thing leads to another, so here it was with Ribas. He had met the Bacorigues and the Bacorigues introduced him to the Comoporis. These lived among the dunes of a lonely peninsula some fifteen miles northwest of Fuerte's mouth, and though they spoke the same language as the Ahomes, they held no bond of friendship and slew them upon slight provocation.

[7]*Ibid.*
[8]*Ibid.*

But after the Ahomes had been converted to the Faith some of
their bolder spirits ventured among these savage peninsulars and
so the glad tidings dribbled in. One of the Ahomes was a man in
whom Ribas placed especial confidence and whom the Comoporis
trusted more than the rest. Here was a good instrument of contact;
Ribas made him his ambassador. This Ahome conveyed to the
savages of the sea that the padre of the Ahomes would be delighted to see them and that, should they come to visit him, they
would be wonderfully treated. The Comoporis arrived one by one
at first, and then in groups, bringing finally even their women.
Ribas pleased them with gifts of varied sort, they witnessed the
ecclesiastical feasts and celebrations of the Christians, and sensed
perhaps most of all the new spirit of happiness which had penetrated the pueblo of their kinsmen. They ended by petitioning
baptism!

For this Ribas must go to them. It was considered dangerous,
but his superiors allowed it provided he would take a body-guard
for his safety. Don Miguel got a group together who were proud
to be protectors of their padre. Some ugly rumors had got afloat
that the Comoporis were meditating treachery, and Ribas became
somewhat disturbed. But to show any sign of fear would have
lowered his prestige, nor did he see any excuse under cover of
which he could gracefully withdraw from the arrangements already
made.

Saying Mass before break of day, Ribas set out very early to
the rendezvous agreed upon with his Ahome guard. What was
his surprise to find not a couple of dozen, but a hundred Ahome
braves ready to make the journey with him to the coast. Ribas
protested to Don Miguel. Such a number would irritate the Comoporis and lead them to suspect inimical intent. The missionary
writes that Don Miguel made the following reply: "I know,
father, and I selected only the number you had asked for. But
these your sons said they had slight faith in the Comoporis. They
knew these people well and had no desire to see their father run
the risk of being slain. It was impossible to keep them from
coming."[9] If Ribas reports without exaggeration this was a grand

[9]Ribas, III, 8.

reply to his protests and so they set out. Added guarantee for the padre's safety was the fact that there was present among them an Indian lad of eighteen, distinguished for his horsemanship and bravery, protégé of Captain Hurdaide. This day he was representing the Captain himself. He showed up on horseback, and because he had no Spanish armor he painted arms upon himself with Indian red and daubed his horse with the same color. This lad Ribas sent ahead with messages of peace.

The company of Ahomes with Ribas crossed the Fuerte near its mouth and then trudged miles up along the coast, until finally they came to the country of the Comoporis. There was no sign of a pueblo, for these people lived wild upon the land. Their chief Cohari came up with a group of warriors, reassuringly small. But, not an encouraging sign, the women were absent. Ribas asked after them, saying he had brought them sweetmeats and gifts. The women were away fishing, according to Cohari, and later some came up carrying fish and oysters they had just taken from the sea. Chief Cohari showed the padre over all his lands and pointed out the bays and coves best for fishing. Towards the end of the day the chief of his own accord brought the conversation around to religion, and Ribas was able to begin his apostolic work with the cacique himself.

It had been arranged to stay the night. An enramada had been prepared for Ribas' comfort. His faithful Ahomes were on the alert; they still suspected treachery. A special guard kept watch that night near the enramada and the others farther off lit fires to keep an eye upon the approaches. But nothing happened and the morning proved their fears had been unfounded. For the women came up with the men in friendly mood and all were delighted with the gifts which Ribas dispensed to them. Thus the second day passed pleasantly until it was time to depart.

On leaving, the company passed a place where a pile of bones was heaped at the foot of some upright poles. The chief explained that the bones were of those who had been slain by sharks at different times as the victims were fording a small arm of the sea. This reverence done the bones of the dead would protect the living from a like calamity. Ribas decried the superstition, explained that all trust should be placed only in the one true God. He then ordered his Ahomes to throw down the poles and bury the bones. Though Chief Cohari at first paled with fear at this insult to the Great Spirit, still when nothing happened, when the men who destroyed the sacred spot still lived and Ribas did not die, Cohari recognized his superstition and came one step closer to acceptance of faith in the God of the Ahomes.[10]

This was the beginning. The Comoporis went in ever greater numbers to visit the Ahomes and to participate in the Christian rites. A few began to ask for baptism. Ribas paid the Comoporis other visits; taught them how to sow grain and to live in less barbarous fashion. Within two years' time the whole tribe had accepted Christianity, and Ribas had baptized them all. It was another triumph of the Faith, to demonstrate which to the world our missionary was going to write a great book.

---

[10] *Ibid.*

CHAPTER VI

Suaqui Chiefs Do Penance

The time finally came when Ribas judged the adults of the Suaqui tribe to be ready for the holy waters. They had been assiduous in attending his instructions twice a day when he was among them and those of his interpreter and catechist, Luisa, when he was absent. They had replaced in their two pueblos the first rude and flimsy chapels with more substantial structures though not so pretentious as that which the Ahomes had built with such pride. Brigandage, which used to be their normal occupation and the almost continual subject of their conversation, was now entirely dropped by them. They would come touchingly to the padre and express their happiness at his being among them. In due time, therefore, Ribas judged it safe to proceed with the baptism of the adults.

Wisely he would begin with the caciques. In their chiefs the Suaquis were different from the Ahomes. These latter were a much smaller group of not many hundreds, all centered about one pueblo under one cacique, Don Pedro, and his son who succeeded him, Don Miguel, who was so great a help to Ribas in all his work. But among the Suaquis there were many such to whom the tribe looked for leadership. This is why Hurdaide went so far to subdue the Suaqui tribe in 1601 when he captured and slew forty-two of these leaders. It was a smart gesture, therefore, now to begin the baptisms of adults with what were left of the chiefs, for with these as Christians the rest would easily follow. There would be just one difficulty: they were polygamists all of them, and it would be the strongest proof of Ribas' ability and prestige could he, after pouring the waters of baptism, restrain them successfully to one wife.

This actually the missionary accomplished and this assured the permanent conversion of the whole Suaqui tribe. Venturo, who had escaped the vengeance of Hurdaide, was one of the first to be baptized. Another cacique, unnamed, was led to Christian chastity and to baptism in the following manner. He came one day with his little boy to greet Ribas. He began to raise the father's hand to kiss it. But Ribas drew back saying he did not

31

wish to be thus honored by one who was keeping two wives and who would not become a Christian as his fellows were doing. The result was what had been expected. The chief thus humbled and perhaps fearing to lose face with his followers, dismissed one of his wives and thus came to petition baptism. It was readily conceded. He was baptized and forthwith married to his wife with the blessing of the Church.[1]

There was one of large prestige whom Ribas was particularly anxious to win over. He was the principal cacique, seeming to enjoy more authority than the rest. By a deed of valor in war he had gained the reputation of great bravery and among the Suaquis he was a power for good or evil. His name was Anamei. He possessed many wives, but so great was the influence to which Ribas had now attained that Anamei became willing to receive baptism even though it meant the dismissal of all his women except the one to be his legitimate wife. So was it done. He was baptized together with the one whom he had chosen for his permanent companion and then he was married to her through the rites of the Church. He was given a Christian name and was appointed by Hurdaide, as was the case with Don Miguel at Ahome, official governor for Spain of all the Suaquis. He was given a sword, he wore the Spanish dress and he enjoyed a grand title, being known thereafter as Don Cristóbal Anamei. Ribas was fond of this man. "He was," says the missionary, "a wonderful influence for all the nation and the strong support of the fathers, governing thus his people until death."[2]

But the new life was not entirely easy for Chief Anamei, and once at least shortly after his baptism he broke over the traces. While at the pueblo of another tribe he seized the wife of a Christian and made off with her. The thing was serious enough, for though no one dared to take vengeance upon him, if the crime went unpunished it would lower morale immediately and other caciques would consider themselves thus privileged. Hurdaide approached by Ribas, who thought Anamei should be punished, was afraid of rebellion should he proceed against the chief.

---

[1]Ribas, III, 12.
[2]Ibid.

But soon the problem was solved by Don Cristóbal himself. He came at midnight shortly after his crime and demanded of the boy who served the padre and who was sleeping near the door of the church to see Ribas. Admitted, the chief fell to his knees, expressed sorrow for his sin and offered to do a penance. Ribas showed his usual wisdom; he mitigated the penance, but made it public since the sin had been public. He had the boy summon from their slumber the fiscals of the pueblo. Before them as witnesses Cristóbal proceeded to his penance. He removed his coat and shirt, dropped to his knees, and began to flog himself before the padre, the two fiscals, and the boy. Ribas stopped him shortly and the affair was over.[3]

The whole tribe of the Suaquis followed the example of their caciques, and when the baptisms were completed three thousand souls had been added to the membership of the Church Universal.[4] With all the Suaquis now in the fold it was high time to proceed to the construction of more substantial churches, similar to the fabric at San Felipe on the Sinaloa and to that of the Ahomes. Two were needed for the Suaquis, one for each of their pueblos. From the description which their missionary gives of the larger of these churches built in their larger pueblo of Mochicahue, it surpassed that of Ahome. Four hundred, sometimes six hundred, individuals at one time were engaged in its construction, employed in the various activities far and near of getting down great timbers from the mountains which would sustain the roof, of gathering and plaiting the osiers for this latter, of shaping and baking the adobes, of organizing and forming all these into a fabric which would be enduring and at the same time good to look upon.

When the building was finished the savages were proud of their work. It enjoyed a fine facade which was whitewashed. Some yards in front of it a large cross was erected which marked the plaza and the cemetery. A merry celebration was planned for the day of dedication. The psychology of Ribas on such an occasion was good. He writes: "Great care was taken to solemnize these festive occasions with all that made for pageantry and joy. In our

---

[3]Ribas, III, 13.
[4]Ribas, III, 12.

happiness to have witnessed the spiritual conquest of the valorous Suaquis, all the more difficult because of the hold the demon had upon them, nothing was spared in the way of music, games, dances, and bonfires for the joy of the people of this poor land."[5]

A rocky hillock rose hard by the level upon which the church was built. Here a statute of the Virgin Mary was placed and on the day of dedication two groups of musicians played in turn from the summit of this hill and from the roof of the church. Streamers of silk, come all the way from China via the Philippines, lent their color to the occasion. At night there were fires lit on the plaza; there was dancing and universal joy. The following day a procession marched about the church and through the plaza in front, stopping for prayer at bowers set up at regular intervals. At each of these was an altar and a carpet of leaves. Mass followed the procession. A missionary from a neighboring pueblo preached a sermon and there were guests innumerable. After Mass the Suaquis were regaled with gifts of food, delicacies of beef and fish, brought up to them by the Ahomes.[6]

What Martín Pérez had effected at Sinaloa, what Pedro Méndez had done at Ocoroni, Ribas brought about at Ahome and at Mochicahue. He organized a school for his young neophytes where with assistants he taught them to read Spanish, to write, and to sing in the services of the church. These missions of Pérez de Ribas were not very old before the Mass could be well sung by the boys' choir, and musical instruments of various kinds used for the enhancement of the religious service. Through the spread of such work among the Indians all along the west coast illiteracy was lessened and a goodly vein of European culture was introduced.

Thus was the Black Robe successful in bringing the whole tribe of the Suaquis, as well as the Ahomes, within the fold of the Church. This was exactly what his confréres farther up the river were likewise successfully accomplishing, Méndez among the Tehuecos and Villalta among the Sinaloas. And thus the whole length of Río Fuerte from where it slips out of the deep canyons

---

[5]*Ibid.*
[6]*Ibid.*

of the Sierra Madre to where it drops into the western sea was being refined by the culture of Christianity.

As for Mochicahue, the hill hard by the ruins of the ancient church, upon whose summit the shrine of Our Lady had been set, still dominates the immediate country and from its brow one can gaze upon the landscape east and west where Ribas worked. Upon its rocky summit a small mound of mouldering earth still indicates the ancient spot where once stood the Suaqui shrine of Blessed Mary the Virgin.

CHAPTER VII

LAST YEARS ON THE FUERTE

The whole career of Ribas was thrown upon times of progress and expansion, excepting possibly the last few years of his life. Certainly his missionary career coincided with a great and glorious period. The presence of a new arrival at Tehueco, Father Laurentín Adame, indicates that the number of Black Robes in Sinaloa was being increased. A high-born and famous Jesuit, Father Pedro de Velasco, son of the Viceroy Luis de Velasco II, came to the missions in 1607 and soon began working on the upper Sinaloa where he achieved a resounding success. In 1611 the Bishop of far-off Guadalajara, five hundred miles to the south, made the arduous journey north to visit the new Christians of Nueva Vizcaya, which lay in his vast diocese. After seeing the Jesuit missions of Durango and of the plains east of the Sierra Madre he crossed the mountains to Sinaloa which was the extreme northwestern part of his diocese. The Bishop's name was Juan del Valle and he was a Benedictine.[1]

The Bishop's visit to the mother mission of San Felipe was a matter of great importance and consolation to Pérez de Ribas and to all the fathers. Eight thousand neophytes were confirmed on this occasion and several thousands of these would come down from Río Fuerte. Ribas would lead up his faithful Ahomes, his Suaquis, and his sea Indians, the Batucaris, the Bacorigues, and the Comoporis. A safe guess would be that Ribas led to confirmation about a thousand from the Suaquis and almost a thousand from the Ahomes and the other tribes near the sea. Ribas, too, would be one of those called in to help. So great was the press of savages seeking the sacrament that clergy and laity, soldier and padre, were called upon to assist the Bishop and to aid in the preservation of order. Ribas thus describes the event: "For five days, morning and afternoon, the Bishop labored. Two or three fathers were always in attendance, helping the soldiers keep order among the Indians, instructing those who were backward, exhorting all to fervor, and trying to put into some sort of condition

---

[1]Ribas, III, 16.

those who came in rags or almost entirely naked to the sacrament. White cotton gowns were ready for the purpose. But no matter how ill-clad some appeared, the Bishop received them kindly, for he was a benign father, and even when in the press of humanity some dropped down before him almost totally unclothed, he confirmed them also as they were."[2] The Bishop gave instructions to the soldiers who were keeping order that they refuse no one to come to him and that they give no cause of displeasure.[3]

If this visit and the confirming of the neophytes was of exceeding consolation to Pérez de Ribas and the other missionaries, it was equally so to the Bishop. The annual report of 1611 mentions the joy and delight of Del Valle and bespeaks his affection for the Society of Jesus.[4] Ribas himself in his *Los Triumphos* quotes the Bishop's letter to the Jesuit Provincial, Rodrigo de Cabredo: "I have seen almost all the fathers of those missions, from which I return greatly consoled and greatly edified. For it has appeared clearly to me how much the Church, His Majesty, and the Society owe to these fathers for the notable progress they have made in those districts and for the great sufferings they endure among their savage charges. Wherever I shall go I shall have to be the herald of the fathers and of the good things which I have seen and touched. . . . And so far as I can I shall be the great protector of these missions and of the fathers who labor in them."[5]

The year 1615, beginning the eleventh for Ribas on the Fuerte, was the last complete twelve months he would spend upon the river. The following year he would make a business trip to Mexico City and in 1617 he would be assigned to begin the missions on the Yaqui.

But this year of 1615 an event occurred to break the even and perhaps at times monotonous routine of missionary life on the lower Fuerte. Indians who had been down to the coast came up excitedly one day to Ribas and reported an extraordinary vision: they had seen a tall white thing at sea, a palace swimming on the wave. The report sped over the land and soon all knew of it. The

---

[2]*Ibid.*
[3]*Ibid.*
[4]*Anua* of 1611, *Memorias*, p. 449.
[5]Ribas, III, 16.

simple savage went down in droves to the sea to gaze upon the unique phenomenon; their padre remained at home and speculated upon the event.

Pérez de Ribas was a scholar as well as a missionary. He knew that from the time of Cortés Spaniards had ventured into the Gulf of California to explore its coasts and to seek for treasure. He knew that the men of Cortés had pierced into the Gulf of California, that Ulloa had sailed in 1539 up to the very end of the Gulf and that Alarcón the following year had even penetrated several hundred miles up the Colorado River. Ribas knew likewise that the freebooter and the pirate had prowled over those waters, having followed the course of the great Magellan through the Straits. Sir Francis Drake had appeared off Lower California shores in 1579, and in 1586 Thomas Cavendish lay in wait near these same waters for the Manila galleon, the *Santa Ana,* swinging down the coast to Acapulco. Cavendish plundered the *Santa Ana* and burnt it. The Dutch here as elsewhere around the globe followed in the wake of the English and before the sixteenth century had run its course, almost a decade before Ribas had come to the Fuerte, Dutch pirates had sailed into the waters of California's gulf. The Spaniards called them Pichilingues. Indeed, at this very time the Dutch freebooter, Spillberg, was prowling about these seas, but Ribas knew it not.[6]

Because, therefore, no reports of pirates had come to him the missionary at Ahome surmised, and indeed correctly, that what his Indians had seen was a vessel of some Spanish seamen. He thought to send them a letter of information, telling them on what coasts they were and what manner of people lived upon them. He wrote this letter. He said that he was a Spanish Jesuit missionary, that he had lived now for ten years near this edge of the sea among faithful and peaceable Indians whom he had partly recalled from their savage state. He gave this letter to a trustworthy Ahome whom he knew to be a good swimmer and imparted his instructions. The swimmer was to go down immediately to the coast and remain there watching for the appearance of that house upon the water. Should it be in sight he was to roll the letter

<hr>

[6]Cf. Bolton and Marshall, pp. 44, 45, 70 and 240.

into a hollow piece of wood, seal it watertight, tie it to his hair and swim out to the floating palace to deliver the message to the men who lived in it.

But interesting things happened before this could be accomplished. A day or so after these events, while Ribas was resting at Ahome, he heard a bustle of excitement and beheld two Spaniards, wan and emaciated, approaching his dwelling. They were surrounded by a crowd of his curious neophytes. The surprise was mutual. That they should find a priest, a Jesuit padre, here alone among savages on this lonely and isolated coast—this was like an apparition, it was something like the joy of homecoming after wild adventures. Ribas soon got their story. They were of the crew of Captain Juan Iturbi, commissioned under royal patent by Tomás Cardona of Seville, to hunt for pearls on the Caribbean Sea and along the coasts of the Gulf of California. They told Ribas their party had rounded the Horn in two ships, a frigate and a pinnace, and had reached the tip of California's peninsula, Cape San Lucas, where they met with a Dutch pirate who captured and looted the frigate.

Though they did not know it, the pearl fishers had fallen into the tender arms of Spillberg, and their expedition and adventure became well known in the history of the west coast.[7] The purpose of the Spaniards in coming ashore was to hunt for provisions. Their supplies had run out and they were in a precarious condition. Their captain had thus ordered them ashore to search for food.

Ribas was delighted to help these fellow countrymen. He took them in and fed them just as two hundred years later in Alta California the Franciscan missionaries welcomed and entertained the American trapper Jedediah Smith. This padre of the seventeenth century was happy to place before his guests the modest fare of his establishment. It was not so abundant nor so luxurious as what the later Franciscans in the north were to be able to proffer the tired traveler. But to the hungry Spaniards it was probably the best food they had ever before tasted. Ribas regaled them with

---

[7]*Ibid.*, p. 240; Alegre, III, 77; Orozco y Berra, *Apuntes para la Historia de la Geografía en México*, p. 178; Venegas (French edition), I, 229, etc.; Caughey, *California*, pp. 103ff., gives a good running account of this and similar visits of pearl fishers to the coasts of Lower California.

jerked beef, tortillas, frijoles, and corn; with these viands their hunger was driven out.

Next morning Pérez de Ribas and his Spanish guests with many Indians set out for the coast to save from starvation the captain of the vessel and his crew. Don Miguel, at Ribas' request, had gathered and was transporting with his men a goodly store of provisions for this purpose. Pack-mules were laden with the food. A great crowd of Indians followed, who like children were anxious to witness all that was going on.

The two Spaniards could not find the spot where they had anchored their small boat and all day was spent in hunting for it. Finally towards evening it was discovered, and as the pack-animals could not make their way through the swamps the provisions had to be carried by the Indians. Finally the well-laden skiff made off to the ship. The missionary and his party tarried there another night and the following day the skiff returned carrying an invitation for Ribas and some of his neophytes to visit the craft. So it was done. A row of about two miles brought them to the anchored vessel. Here the party was joyfully entertained by Captain Iturbi who in turn received from Ribas valuable information concerning the harbor of Sinaloa some seventy miles south where, the captain was informed, he could get in touch with Hurdaide, who would gladly tender aid in all things necessary.[8]

The ship remained two or three days in the offing, during which time the Indians did not cease to visit the Spaniards, exchanging the produce of their fields for goods the Spaniards were able to offer. Ribas and his Ahomes finally withdrew to their pueblo and Captain Iturbi sailed away south to seek Hurdaide and the port at the mouth of Río Sinaloa.

The whole episode had a fine effect upon Ribas' neophytes. On the way home they said to him: "Father, now we are confirmed in all the doctrines of the Church which you have preached to us, because we see with our own eyes what you have often told us, that you have come from your own country to preach to us the law of God, crossing the sea in a floating house. Now we have

---

[8]Alegre, II, 77f; Ribas, III, 10.

seen it with our own eyes."[9] The missionary was highly satisfied with the effects of this whole affair. For the Faith which he had preached it was a windfall of spiritual fruit, for himself it had been a delightful break in the evenness of his solitary existence.

This was the last noted episode concerning Pérez de Ribas during his almost eleven years' happy and fruitful residence on Río Fuerte. Soon he would be called away to other fields to build the structure of other missions and to witness the still farther advance of the Spanish and ecclesiastical frontier.[10]

---

[9]Ribas, *loc. cit.*

[10]Iturbi succeeded in meeting Hurdaide who wrote to the Viceroy for instructions. Iturbi was to set out immediately to meet the Manila galleon and accompany it to Acapulco.

CHAPTER VIII

On to Río Yaqui

The year of grace 1616 was eventful for the Jesuit missions on the west coast as well as for the life-story of Andrés Pérez de Ribas. Late in that year there flared forth the tragic Tepehuán revolt of the Tepehuán Indians against their missionaries, the Jesuit fathers. The uprising bore devastating effect east of the Sierra Madre mountains taking toll of hundreds of Spanish lives.[1] Sparks from this general conflagration east were to be blown over the cordillera and to fall upon the missions west. Most fortunately, Captain Diego Martínez de Hurdaide was present to extinguish them before they ignited a flame to the destruction likewise of the western missions.

The year was eventful likewise for Ribas. It was to be his last on the Fuerte, nor would he finish out 1616 among his Suaquis and Ahomes. The Mayos had waited long for their missionaries. The padres came to them finally in 1614. Now it was six years since the Yaquis, finally tamed, had asked for their own Black Robes. After routing Hurdaides' army in 1609, the Yaquis became conciliated the following year, while their leaders desired to become incorporated into the Spanish mission system. After 1614 when the Jesuits Pedro Méndez and Diego de la Cruz went to the Mayos, the Yaquis began to press more insistently that they too might have their padres. Indeed, they showed all the indications of jealousy over the Mayos' happy lot. Neither Captain Hurdaide, nor Martín Pérez, Superior at San Felipe, nor any other of the missionaries would be indifferent to the desires of the valorous Yaquis.

A meeting was therefore held in the summer of 1616 to discuss the question of missionaries for the Yaqui tribe. Captain Hurdaide, Martín Pérez, and several other Jesuits made up the consultation. It was decided to send one of the missionaries to Mexico City to plead with the Viceroy for the extension of the missions and the frontier to the Yaquis on Río Yaqui. These savages had during the past six years proved their friendship for the Spaniards and their readiness for the Faith. They should

---

[1]Ribas, X, 13ff.

42

not be kept waiting longer. One of the padres, therefore, was chosen to make the journey to Mexico City, and the lot fell upon Pérez de Ribas himself.[2]

To advance to another river, to extend the frontier another sixty or seventy miles permission of the Viceroy must be obtained. Under the regime of the *Patronato Real* or Royal Patronage, the Church in New Spain, indeed as in Spain itself, was ruled from Madrid. It was not the Pope, therefore, who designated the bishops in the vast Spanish colonies of the Americas, or who created new dioceses, or who sent the missionaries of the various religious orders. It was the King who did all this, governing even the Church in the New World through that powerful body known as the Council of the Indies. This arrangement had developed gradually during the later Middle Ages, with the permission or the connivance (sometimes a necessary connivance) of the Papacy. The Viceroy, therefore, in Mexico City representing the King of Spain, at this time Philip III, must be consulted not only for the extension of Spain's political frontier up to the Yaqui River, but likewise for the advance to this point of the mission system.

But, as a matter of fact, both went together, and it was a commonplace at this time in Mexico that the one could not advance without the other; the frontier needed the mission. Just as Captain Hurdaide traveled to Mexico City in 1599 and again in 1604 in the interests of this frontier of Sinaloa, so now it was agreed among the Captain and the fathers that Pérez de Ribas should depart south on the same business. He was to do two things: obtain permission to advance the frontier to the Yaqui River and, succeeding in this, obtain added missionaries that the new district be able to be manned.

Ribas departed on his long journey early in September, 1616.[3] It was a retracing of his steps of twelve years ago when first he came to the missions of the west coast. South to Culiacán, then east into the heart of the Sierra Madre through Tamazula to Topia, still east through deep defiles and rugged arroyos threading the divide into more open country where he would

---

[2] Ribas, V, 6.
[3] Alegre, II, 92.

reach the mission Santa Catalina among the Tepehuanes. The same mule-path is traveled today after three centuries, for no wagon-road has ever crossed these torn and crumpled mountains. Descending a lovely stream, the Río Tepehuanes, along a verdant valley Ribas would come to another mission, Santiago Papasquiaro. Crossing a barrier of hills and turning south he would emerge onto the broad plain of Durango and from there his route would be southeast to Zacatecas and then on to Mexico City.

Issuing from the gorges and defiles of the high sierra going east Ribas found himself again in Jesuit mission country or rather did he just pass from one province of the Jesuit mission system to another. Here east of the mountains the Black Robes had labored and organized among the savage just as they had done in the west, not however with the same resounding success owing to the different and at times more difficult quality of the Indians. Juan Agustín de Espinosa started the evangelization of the Lagunero Indians in the more central plains in 1594; while in 1596 Gerónimo Ramírez started missionary labors among the Tepehuanes fifty and a hundred miles north and northwest of Durango.[4] These missions had flourished and spread and by 1616 seven fathers were working among the Tepehuanes alone. Santa Catalina, the first of this group touched by Ribas had no resident missionary, but Santiago Papasquiaro, nestled in delightful country and sitting on the banks of its clear flowing Río de Santiago, enjoyed the ministrations of Diego de Orozco and Bernardo de Cisneros.

Ribas arrived here sometime towards the end of September and spent several days with his two confrères. Always wide-awake and observing, Ribas had felt and noted a difference in the personality of these Tepehuán Indians. It is true, these people were far from being the affectionate and gentle type of his Ahomes whom he loved so well, nor were they ever so warm-hearted as the enthusiastic Mayos whom he had known in the west. But his impression now was still more unfavorable. This feeling deepened when he accepted the invitation of Orozco and Cisneros to accompany them on a visit to several of the pueblos.

---

[4] Ribas, X, 2.

Ribas says of this experience: "And here I shall write what I saw with my own eyes. . . . That visit produced in me two effects. One was the novelty of these people in which there did not exist that love for the Church (generally speaking) which we were accustomed to experience in our Christian natives of Sinaloa. Neither did they have nor did they manifest that tincture of Christianity, nor that respect and good will towards the fathers which was enjoyed elsewhere." Nor did Ribas keep his thoughts and feelings to himself. "I signified my impressions to the father who accompanied me and he replied: 'Who knows what demon of an idol has come into this nation to render it changed and restless. We spare no possible effort to help and quiet this people, I and the other fathers.' Thus did Father Bernardo Cisneros reply, one of the eight who two months later died at the hands of the rebellious Tepehuanes."[5]

These are weighty words of our missionary-historian. It may be that he sensed the spirit of revolt among the sullen Tepehuanes, and left for the south with the worst of forebodings. In any case, he was not gone many weeks when the smouldering discontent broke forth into a flame which destroyed the Tepehuán mission and consumed the lives of ten missionaries and about three hundred colonials.[6]

Years later in the tenth book of his *Los Triumphos* Ribas was to write the detailed history of this the greatest and most murderous rebellion which the Jesuits in all the history of the Americas were ever called upon to endure. The Iroquois in Canada or New France would after three decades put to death six Jesuits, including St. Isaac Jogues who fell in October, 1646, almost exactly thirty years after the events we are relating.

In 1616, in the middle of November, two months after Ribas parted from their midst, Cisneros and Orozco at Santiago Papasquiaro; Del Valle and Alabez, Fonte and Moranta, all at Zape, fell at the hands of their own neophytes. They were slain outright with arrows, clubs, or hatchets together with hundreds of

---

[5]Ribas, X, 12.

[6]For a detailed account of the revolt cf. Dunne, *Pioneer Jesuits in Northern Mexico*, ch. XIII to XVII; also a briefer account by the same, "The Tepehuán Revolt," *Mid-America*, XVIII, (Jan., 1936), 3-14.

Spaniards and their slaves or servants. The exception was Orozco who was briefly tortured before his death. Felled first by arrows, two savages held him up in the form of a cross while another sliced and hacked his flesh till he died. Two Jesuit visitors to the mission, Hernando de Tovar and the illustrious Santarén also fell, murdered in a strange country. A Franciscan and a Dominican were likewise slain.

Leaving the missions, Ribas made his way to Durango to confer with Don Gaspar de Alvear, Knight of Santiago and Governor of the vast province of Nueva Vizcaya, of which Sinaloa was but a section. Ribas found the Governor cool towards his mission. He had not approved Hurdaide's entradas into Yaqui country, nor did he consider these Indians ready for the gospel. Ribas explains this attitude through Alvear's lack of experience, for only a few months previously he had succeeded Governor Francisco de Urdiñola, a well-seasoned frontiersman.[7]

From Durango Ribas made his way south through Zacatecas to Mexico City to begin negotiations for the inauguration of the new Yaqui mission. Arrived at the capital he lost no time in presenting himself before the Viceroy, Diego Fernández de Córdova, the Marquis of Guadalcázar, and was able to win his enthusiastic support.

Ribas found the Viceroy a great admirer of Captain Hurdaide and was encouraged to discover that the Marquis appraised at its high value what the Captain had been able to accomplish among the Yaquis. The Viceroy gave the Captain full credit for the present peaceful and promising situation on the river. He even asked Ribas to put immediately in writing the whole story of the winning of the Yaquis. This memorial finished, the Viceroy considered its argument in consultation with the members of his chancellery.

The result was a favorable decree issued from the viceregal office, according to which the Yaqui Indians were to be taken under the protection of the King of Spain and their river incorporated into the frontier of the empire of Spain. The Christianization of the tribe was to begin immediately. Captain Hurdaide

7Ribas, X, 12.

was to carry out the civil implications of this decision while two Jesuit fathers were to begin the preaching of the Gospel. Two would be sufficient for the present, the Viceroy thought, and others might be added later. There were two reasons why the Viceroy did not wish to send immediately more than two fathers. Gaspar de Alvear, Governor of Nueva Vizcaya, was not favorable to the idea, and one or another of the Yaqui chiefs was known to be not over friendly.[8]

The Viceroy ordered the officers of the royal exchequer to provide ornaments and fixtures for two altars and bells and musical instruments for the outfitting of two churches. "This," adds Ribas, "in full conformity with the great Catholic piety with which our kings administer the patronage which God and His Vicar gave them over the widely extended ecclesiastical provinces of the New World."[9] The Patronato Real was being administered magnificently for Ribas at the present time and it is right to say that this same generosity of the viceregal government of New Spain was acting in conformity with a long-adopted policy for the encouragement and furtherance of the missions.

The Viceroy communicated to the Jesuit Provincial, Rodrigo de Cabredo, his wish for the augmentation of the manpower of the missions of Sinaloa in order that men could be spared for the Yaqui. The Provincial forthwith made his appointments. The two missionaries for the introduction of the Faith to the Yaqui River were to be Father Tomás Basilio, recently arrived from Spain, and—Andrés Pérez de Ribas himself. Ribas was pleased with the appointment which he considered an honorable one. His suit had been completely successful. He would now exchange the Fuerte and his gentle Ahomes and tamed Suaquis for the still barbarous and slightly doubtful Yaqui Indians.

Fortunately for Ribas and for the Yaqui mission, word of the tragic Tepehuán revolt did not reach the capital until after the fathers had departed. Had the story of the murderous rebellion come to the ears of the officials or of Ribas while he was in Mexico City the news would have dealt a blow to his spirits and

---

[8]Ribas, V, 6.
[9]*Ibid.*

rendered more difficult his work of persuasion and organization. It would have seemed a most unpropitious time to be planning and organizing for the extension of one mission just while another mission was being destroyed by rebellion.

However, neither Pérez de Ribas nor the Jesuit Superior in Mexico City, nor the Viceroy had heard the tragic news of the revolt and of the murders before Ribas departed for the north. The Black Robe himself makes this very clear, and no other available evidence contradicts his testimony.[10] In fact it is probable that Ribas had already left the capital when the revolt broke out, nor did he get word of it until he had traveled almost to Durango.

Since, therefore, Pérez de Ribas and Tomás Basilio knew nothing of the storm about to burst in the north, it was with happy minds and contented hearts that they departed for Sinaloa astride their mounts and followed by a pack train and muleteers. As for Ribas, he was about to open the important Yaqui mission; as for Basilio, he was to begin in this new mission his whole active and hazardous career as missionary in the wilds of the north. Basilio's life would be twice attempted, once by the Yaquis, once by the Nébomes. He would be pierced in the arm by a poisoned arrow and the wound would never heal. He would however baptize his thousands. These things Basilio, traveling north with Ribas, could not foresee. But he was ready for them all. Basilio and Ribas were going soon to play an important part in the development of the west coast of North America

---

[10]Ribas, V, 6.

CHAPTER IX

YAQUIS INVITE RIBAS

Our Black Robe missionary, Pérez de Ribas, together with the novice missioner, Tomás Basilio, departed north from Mexico City sometime near the middle of November, 1616. A cavalcade, not of mighty chargers, but of meek, mild-eyed burros driven by Indian *mozos* and mestizos accompanied the fathers. These pack-animals were laden with the bounty of the Viceroy towards the prospective mission on the Yaqui: two sets of everything needed for divine service—amices, albs, cinctures, and sets of vestments, each set comprising a chasuble, a maniple, and a stole. Indeed, there would be ten sets of vestments, for the travelers were taking with them the fittings and trappings for two altars, and the vestments for each would have to be in the five colors used for the different liturgical feasts and seasons of the ecclesiastical year—white for Easter time; purple during Advent and Lent; red during Pentecost; green on ordinary Sundays and black for Masses of the dead.

Many other things the grey and meek-eyed burros had to carry on their backs: cloths for the altar, three pieces for each; chalices and patens; purificators, corporals, and palls; bells large and small; pictures, vessels for water, antependiums; not to mention vases for flowers, candles and candlesticks. The ever-present crucifix too would be there, prized among the most necessary of all.

The missionaries departing north from the capital always carried presents for the prospective neophyte. So practical a man as Ribas would have a rich variety. Indeed, already in Spain, and, if Germans, already in Germany (for Germans later came to these missions), the missionaries had begun the collection of gifts for their future spiritual children: knives, hatchets, glass beads, medals, rosaries, scapulars, colored string, ribbon, pieces of silk, and other fancy and delectable objects suited for the curious eye of the women, and even for the male Indian who always remained a child. Barrels of wine, of course, would go along for the Mass, medicines fit for all eventualities, and chocolate for the regaling of Indian and missionary alike. Tobacco too would later sometimes be added to the outfit.

49

The King of Spain through the arrangement of the patronato real was good to the missionary at such a time, and the padre was always sure of his three hundred pesos a year, given by the government for his support. Most often the missionary spent part or all of it on his neophytes or for the adornment of the church. It was well, then, for Ribas and Basilio that the Chichimecos, through whose country the padres had to pass going north, had been tamed and Christianized partly by Gonzalo de Tapia thirty years before, shortly previous to Tapia's founding of the first mission in Sinaloa. Now the journey north was safe; formerly it had always been a hazard.

North the Black Robes trudged, therefore, and west through La Paz, Zacatecas, Sombrerete, to Durango, head and center of the missions on the eastern slope of the cordillera. Ribas and Basilio still heard nothing of the revolt and of the murder of eight of their confrères in the Tepehuán country through which they had to pass. Even at Zacatecas, if they stopped there, no untoward tidings came to them. Ribas tells us that not until they were approaching Durango, and had entered, therefore, into the very land of the rebels, did they come into knowledge of the disaster. But even at this they had personal cause for gratitude, for they arrived a week after the murder of the missionaries, and Ribas reflects that had they not been delayed in the capital a week longer than expected, they would have been going through Tepehuán country just in time to be slain, meeting the fate of Tovar and Santarén, who were merely traveling through the land of the Tepehuanes.[1]

At or near Durango they heard the worst, and we could understand the blow it was to their spirits even if Ribas had not himself described his own disappointment, his fears, and his misgivings. In one section north of Topia the country of the Tepehuanes swung west over the divide. Ribas knew this and he was now told that the rebels had fled thither, escaping the hand of Governor de Alvear, into Acaxée country and on to the borders of the tribes of Sinaloa.

Therefore the danger of the possible spread of the revolt was

---

[1]Ribas, V, 6.

now an anguishing worry to Ribas. Sparks from east of the sierra might fly over the divide and ignite inflammable material on the rivers of the west. Indeed, the rebels did try their best to spread the blaze. A group allied themselves with the restless Cahuemetos on the upper Sinaloa and endeavored to persuade the Chicoratos to join them. They displayed the loot they had taken and a bloody shirt which had been worn by one of the murdered Spaniards. Trouble was here prevented by the loyalty of the two caciques, Luis Tutuqui and Pedro Yotoca. The rebels then threatened Tecuciapa and Carantapa in the same district a little south. But the strong arm of Captain Hurdaide here held the Christians firm; it provoked a counter attack and over a hundred loyal neophytes went on the war-path against the rebel Tepehuanes.

The Nuris in the northwest were tampered with and especially did the Tepehuán rebels try to gain over the Yaquis, though not yet Christians, to join them against the Spaniards. The rebels tempted the Yaquis with blankets and fine garments, loot they had taken in the east—visible signs of the rewards of rebellion. As late as March 5, 1617, Hurdaide writes of the continued threat of danger, and he offers plans to the Viceroy for the efficient stamping out of all hostility.[2] Indeed, just two months before this letter was written, two pueblos of the Acaxée Indians in the mountains near Topia had planned an uprising for January 6 with the murder of their missionaries. The thing was quashed by the captain of the presidio at San Andrés. Among the Xiximes, Fathers Gravina and Mallen had to flee to the presidio of San Hipólito. The stir and restlessness of this Tepehuán revolt was felt even far to the east and among the Laguneros of the plains.[3]

Ribas did not at this time know the story of the gory shirt, the rising of the Cahuemetos, the solicitation of the Chicoratos, and the attempted seduction of his own Yaquis with the loot the rebels had taken from the missions of the east. Of course, had he known *all* he would have been consoled: how the Yaquis were to remain loyal and how the strong arm of Hurdaide maintained

---

[2]*Archiv. Gen. Hist.*, t. 316, p. 102, where Hurdaide's letter is given.
[3]Cf. Dunne, *Pioneer Jesuits in Northern Mexico*, ch. XV.

the peace on the fringes of the Tepehuán country, even though
in the mountains some of the Acaxées and Xiximes did rise, as
Ribas was soon himself to experience. But he feared the worst,
as he tells us, and well he might. Therefore with a heavy heart
he arranged to change his route, swinging south to avoid Tepehuán
territory.

The southern detour followed the Río de San Pedro, turned
west with the stream towards the coast, and then led north along
the narrow corridor between the sierra and the sea. This route
would lengthen the journey by some three hundred miles, but
the padres would thus avoid passing through the Tepehuán and
the disturbed Acaxée country. Fathers Ribas and Basilio with
their pack-train did accordingly, their number now augmented
by two more Jesuits. One of these was designated Superior of
the group. They traveled safely down the river to near the sea
a few miles north of Tepic and then turned to follow up the
coast to San Felipe three hundred and fifty miles away. Things
ran smoothly for a while, for the first hundred miles or so going
north along the coast. Then they ran into trouble—some of the
backwash of the revolt.

At Chiametla near their more southern borders the Tepehuán
rebels had attacked and robbed a small company of soldiers who
were accompanying the transportation of three thousand pesos'
worth of goods which Governor de Alvear had sent from Durango
southwest. All the merchandise was lost, while the inhabitants
of the district had been robbed and massacred by the rebels. At
this very time the colonials were living in terror of further attack.
At San Sebastián the inhabitants had fled to their church as to
a stronghold of protection. Ribas now writes something which is
always the delight of the historian. "And now," says he, "I speak
of things of which I was an eye-witness. Traveling that road
with three other fathers on the way to Sinaloa we arrived at
Chiametla. Though it is some leagues distant from the lands of
the Tepehuanes, we found the inhabitants in great fear of assault
from the rebels. Greater fear existed in the town of San Sebastián
which is closer. The Spaniards of both places begged us religious
to remain with them in a time of such danger, when at any

moment the enemy might break in upon them."[4] The Spaniards evidently felt themselves too few successfully to resist an attack, and in their present danger they desired the spiritual consolations which the Jesuit priests could afford them. Ribas continues: "The father who acted as superior ordered me to go to San Sebastián in that work of piety."[5]

They were indeed close upon the trouble and Ribas must have had continued misgivings concerning the new venture on the Yaqui. But for the time being, he delayed the progress of his journey to act in accordance with the request of his superior. At San Sebastián he prepared the Spaniards for danger and even, if it must be, for death. He exhorted them to courage and piety with sermons and he administered to them the sacraments of confession and of Holy Communion. Every night while Ribas was among them the women and children retired to the church for protection while the men kept watch with lighted fires. The four Jesuit wayfarers remained here ten days and then pursued their way north to San Felipe. The morale of the people had been strengthened and good it was so, as the travelers later found out. For soon after the fathers had departed the Tepehuanes fell upon San Sebastián and upon Acaponeta south. They destroyed the church in both places and in Acaponeta a convent of Franciscan friars. Spaniards were murdered.[6]

However, the Jesuit group of four, including Ribas and Basilio, was able to continue its journey north unmolested. As the party approached San Felipe whatever misgivings Ribas may have suffered were allayed. Captain Hurdaide, ever on the watch, always alert to the action of the moment, had ordered a guard of six mounted Spanish soldiers to march down the coast many leagues to meet the approaching Jesuits and escort them safely to San Felipe. Word of their approach had been sent ahead by an Indian runner so that the good news of an added missionary for the Yaqui must have preceded them. To the warm welcome of their arrival was joined the comforting news that things had been quiet on the rivers of the coast. Only on the upper Sinaloa had

---

[4]X, 30.
[5]*Ibid.*
[6]Ribas, X, 30; *anua* of 1616, Ayer Collection, p. 99; Alegre, II, 91.

there been trouble. The Yaquis, in spite of their temptation, had remained in friendship with the Spaniards and the padres.

A consultation over plans and proposals took place upon the arrival of the group. Hurdaide and the fathers again got together. The topics discussed were of a sufficiently serious nature to be maturely weighed before decisions. In the troubled state of the country south and over the mountains east would it be prudent to risk the opening of a new mission and the extension of a new frontier? Would it not be better to wait until the Tepehuán war was over and the rebellion completely crushed? But this would require a long time, possibly years. It was well known, too, that some of the Yaqui chiefs were inimical, which would throw a weight to the balance of possible failure. Still, on the other side, there was the evident and sincere enthusiasm of the larger part of the Yaqui chiefs, who when they heard that Ribas had returned with Basilio journeyed down to San Felipe and begged a speedy opening of the mission. All of these things were weighed in the balance of pro and con.[7]

There were two men who, we can feel sure, were in favor of immediate action, and they were Ribas and Hurdaide. It happened that there was a third and this clinched the matter. The Father Visitor favored the entrada to the Yaqui country without any delay, allowing only for the time needed to complete the arrangements and to give Basilio a little period in which to learn the language. In order to confirm the decision and to strengthen likewise the courage of the two padres the Father Visitor ordered them under the formality of what is called Holy Obedience to go on the mission. They now had no choice unless they would grievously break their solemn vow given to the superior.

Since Basilio was as anxious as Ribas to get at the holy work, they went forward immediately with their plans. First they would advance to the Mayo. Here Basilio would learn the Yaqui language and Ribas, who had not this need since it was similar to that of the Suaquis, would study conditions on the northern river and make the immediate plans and preparations for the entrada. When the Yaquis heard the fathers were now on the Mayo they

---

[7]Ribas, V, 7.

journeyed down in numbers. Friendly chiefs came to urge speedy action, and others who had never seen the Black Robes before referred to them as the Fathers of the Christians, *los padres de los Christianos*.

Some came too who were unfriendly. These asked their tribesmen whether the blood of the missionaries tasted the same as the blood of other Spaniards. The malcontents tried to sow suspicion. "How is it you go without bow and arrow?" asked the suspicious of the friendly; "Hurdaide will come and kill you all!" Events, however, showed that such murmuring and gloomy spirits were well in the minority. Ribas kept in touch with his superiors and wrote back to them all the details of this temporary sojourn among the Mayos.[8]

Finally the order came from San Felipe to advance to Yaqui. It was a great day for Ribas and Basilio. The latter was about to taste missionary activity for the first time; with Ribas it meant the exchange of one river for another, of the gentle Ahomes, whom he loved so well, and the now peaceable Suaquis, for the numerous, the warlike, and formerly inimical Yaqui tribe.

---

[8]*Ibid.*

CHAPTER X

Yaquis Enter the Church

Pérez de Ribas with Tomás Basilio started for their entrada to the Yaqui Indians on Ascension Day, 1617.[1] This moveable feast almost always falls in May. Ribas would be the leader and official superior because of his greater age and experience, which was rational. The two padres without a soldier and without a guard, made the journey from Mayo up to Yaqui and arrived at the first pueblo of the tribe. One of the missionaries on the Mayo, either Méndez or De la Cruz, accompanied the two fathers for a matter of five or six miles. Four Suaquis from among Ribas' former charges went with the fathers to help in the ceremonies and in baptism. Some Mayos joined the party. There was an element of risk and danger in this entrada. The missionary who had gone part way with them says that he felt they were setting their heads upon a block. Each morning he awoke in dreadful suspense lest he hear of the murder of Ribas and Basilio.[2]

But worries were without foundation. The party's arrival at the first and smallest of the Yaqui pueblos was just as consoling and encouraging as had been the entradas Ribas had made in 1605 to the Suaquis and Ahomes. As they neared this settlement of some two hundred families the two missionaries beheld a large group of Yaquis from this and the other villages approaching in a spirit of friendliness and welcome. There were men, women and children, some women with infants in their arms. They had made a shelter or enramada of poles and branches approached by triumphal arches. As the Indians came nearer the fathers saw that each one was carrying a small cross. The natives turned to accompany their missionaries to the shelter and when they came to it they attached the crosses which they were carrying to the poles and the branches of this enramada. These Yaquis showed a spirit of genuine gladness and happiness and when they had assembled at the enramada Ribas addressed them. He told them how the fathers had left their own homes with their riches and

---

[1]Ribas, V, 8, who gives this date himself. Alegre, II, 94, avers that on June 13 Ribas wrote to superiors telling of his successes.
[2]*Ibid.* For all of this story Ribas himself is the eye-witness.

comforts and had traveled far, through many dangers, for the good of Indian souls which are immortal. He instructed them that to the one true God Who created them they would have to render an account of all their life. In order to open Heaven for them, continued Ribas, God had sent His only Son.[3]

At the end of his discourse Ribas reminded the Yaquis of their own petitions with regard to the Christian religion and stated the advisability of beginning straightway with the baptism of the infants. No sooner said than done. The Yaquis were willing thus to inaugurate the reception of their whole tribe into the portals of the Faith. Ribas had donned for the occasion, a surplice, a stole, and a cope. He was therefore all ready for the holy work. He saw that water was at hand and when he made the invitation the mothers who stood about came timidly forward with their children of seven years and under. The missionary mentions these ages, which had been designated by higher authority. Those not older than seven could be considered infants and therefore fit subjects of baptism without instruction.

Two hundred children on this first occasion received the saving waters, and Ribas tells us that the Yaquis stood in admiration of his vestments and of the rite which he performed. And well they might, for the rite is rich in symbolism and graceful in its beauty. They understood well, wrote the missionary, "that this divine laving was not like the ordinary one they were accustomed to perform in their river."[4]

At nightfall the two fathers went to the huts prepared for them and once they were within, it was impossible to come out because of the press of savage humanity which kept milling about, all curious and excited over the novelty of having the padres now actually in their midst. The Yaquis, wishing to be good hosts to the fathers, brought in to them for their evening repast the best productions of their soil—corn and squash and melons of different kinds. But the Indians also were feasting because this was a great and glorious occasion for them. The pueblo was filled with strangers and the houses of the caciques were filled with people.

---

[3]*Ibid.*
[4]*Ibid.*

There was savage music and whooping, there was dancing, there was speechmaking, and clouds of tobacco smoke were wafted away in the evening breeze which ran calmly over the village.

We can here appreciate the position of the missionary; we have here an example of what occurred over and over again. Ribas and Basilio were tired. They had spent all morning and a goodly part of the afternoon in travel which brought them to this first pueblo. They had to greet the Indians, to be alert and cheerful; Ribas had to make a speech and then come to the labor of two hundred baptisms. They had fully earned their rest that evening and above all, in view of the hard and busy day ahead, they needed sleep. But this it was impossible to enjoy, for all night long the hubbub continued, so that while they fared well in food, they were unable to partake of "the chief nourisher of life's feast." The Yaquis continued celebrating, says Ribas, "with such uproar the whole night long that although we stood in great need of repose it was impossible to obtain it."[5]

It would be a surprising thing if the sorcerer or hechicero, constant thorn in the side of the missionaries, was not present here to try to impede the success of the Black Robes' activity. He *was* present and he *did* do his evil work. But he was not a Yaqui. A Mayo wizard had come up in the company the day of their arrival all unknown to the missionaries. During the night he began to sow his cockle, whispering into the ear of the timid and superstitious women words of suspicion and distrust. Baptism, said he, had always been fatal to the children. If the mothers wanted their babies to die soon why then the best way was to have them baptized. This produced the usual pernicious effect upon the simple and suspicious savage mind. The next morning when the remainder of the babies were to be baptized no one came up at all for the rite, not a mother or baby was to be seen. They had made off to their cornfields and there they held aloof in fear.

The Yaqui chiefs well knew the reason why and they spoke encouragingly to Ribas about it. They explained what had happened and mentioned the timidity of their squaws. But things would work out, they explained. Those babies whom it was im-

---
[5]*Ibid.*

possible to gather up now would all be made ready for the padre
upon his return to this village. The other pueblos were expecting him, they said, and it was advisable not to disappoint them.[6]

So it was done. After three days they moved down the river
to visit, each in its turn, the pueblos of Tesamo, Báhcun, and two
others. It is true, the poison of the Mayo wizard had reached
here and it did have an effect upon the women who, reflects
Ribas, although savages, loved their children. Nevertheless, the
crowds which came out in each to greet the Black Robes were
large and genuinely enthusiastic. The chiefs exerted themselves
to have everything pass in good order and to prepare for a large
number of baptisms. Then, too, the very appearance and speech
of Ribas tended strongly to allay any fear the wizard might have
injected. For it pleased the Yaquis immensely to behold an utter
stranger, such as Ribas, come among them with ease and affabil-
ity and above all with such facility in the speaking of their language. When the mothers saw their chiefs so enthusiastic about
the strangers they were willing to dismiss a great part of their
suspicion. But not all of it. The baptisms, indeed, proceeded
merrily by the two and three hundred count, but it was noticed
that some of the mothers, as the ceremony progressed, wiped off
the salt from the lips of their offspring after a pinch had been
deposited there by Ribas as part of the rite. The Suaqui Indians
who had accompanied the fathers north acted as godparents to
this new flock of little Christians and their spiritual progeny became numerous indeed. Ribas, of course, all during these days
is the leader and takes the more active part. Basilio, for lack of
facility with the language, was at a great disadvantage. But he
may have performed his share of the baptisms.

Following the course of Ribas down the pueblos towards the
lower Yaqui through the reading of his own narrative, and
noting his own comments on the events which took place, the
historian learns two things. He gains a ready insight into much
of the Indian mind and emotion and beholds in the missionary
himself a man of broad intelligence who is able rightly to understand and successfully to manipulate this psychology. Ribas tells

---

[6]*Ibid.*

how at Báhcun the Indians brought to the missionaries tortillas
of maize, besides squash and melon, as they had done at the first
pueblo. This was fine and good because the padres had to live.
But it was somewhat disconcerting that the donors of the food
would not depart until they had seen it consumed by their guests.
Troops of Indians squatted about their hut to watch the padres
eat. The missionaries had to submit to it for this was customary
among the native and he must not by any means be hurt. They
are children, comments Ribas, and it is necessary to treat them
with the greatest patience and the most constant kindness. He
illustrated by an incident.

The pueblos lower down the stream were not as friendly as
those farther up, the chiefs informed Ribas. One day while he
was engaged in a certain work (he does not specify) the press of
savages about him became very great to his embarrassment and
annoyance. He asked them to give way a little that he might
enjoy more freedom of action. Some became offended at this and
averred that they would return to the lower river and say to
their tribesmen there that the padre has no good heart. This in
their mode of thought was as much as to say that Ribas was
not interested, did not love them.[7]

It was during these days that the chiefs explained to Ribas the
reason of their protracted enmity against the Spaniards and their
Captain Hurdaide. It was much the same reason as the Suaquis
had given the missionary years before. They became poisoned
against the Spaniards, the Yaqui chiefs explained, through what
the Ocoroni rebels, Lautaro and Babilonio, had told them during
their sojourn after the rebellion at Ocoroni. These men had re-
counted all sorts of evils to the Yaquis as consequent upon the
Spanish conquest, so that the Yaquis had resolved, proud of their
valor, to shut out such things from the banks of their river.

Thus closes the first chapter of Ribas' successful entrada among
the Yaquis. During these opening days in the four pueblos a
good thousand of infants and other small children were bap-

---

[7]Ribas, V, 9. Compare the lapse from former loyalty, after ten years
of fine Christian spirit, of the Montana Flathead Indians for reasons not
entirely clear. Cf. Garrighan, *The Jesuits of the Middle United States*, II,
375ff.

tized and also a few adults whom for good reasons it was thought well to include. This was the first fruit of Ribas' arduous visit to Mexico City the year before.

The last years of our padre's missionary career were destined to be spent upon the banks of this abundant stream which flows down from the north. They would be happy and fruitful years; but they would not be as equable and uneventful as those spent among the gentle Ahomes and the tame Suaquis. In one way, however, these years would be far more satisfactory. They would witness the marching of the Faith and the extension of the frontier far up Yaqui's stream and the last of these years would inaugurate the most prosperous period in all the history of these missions, not only in point of numbers baptized but also in point of tribes and nations contacted and extent of territory covered. The council at San Felipe and the Father Visitor had been correct; it was fine and good that the entrada to Yaqui be not delayed.

Ribas and Basilio at this time continued downstream and baptized in all the pueblos which the missionary says were eleven. There were hazards on the lower Yaqui. At Abasorin the life of Basilio was attempted and Tórin showed itself not over friendly. But all crises passed and Ribas was pleased with his successes. As he returned upstream Indian mothers would hold up their babies saying: "Look, here is the one you baptized." The Black Robe knew by this that these children of the wild understood the significance of spiritual relationship. His heart was warmed and his spirit knew the sweetness of spiritual paternity.

CHAPTER XI

RIBAS CONSOLIDATES

Andrés Pérez de Ribas returned then to the upper river to consolidate the gains he had made upon it. There were two important things to do: organize for the building of churches as on the Fuerte River and prepare the adults for baptism.

As for the churches, the Yaquis had been more remiss in this preparation than the tribes of the Fuerte. The Ahomes and the Suaquis had built in expectation of the padre's coming temporary structures of larger proportions than any they had made for their own homes. These were called *grandes xacales* (now spelled *jacales*), to distinguish them from their own ordinary jacales or huts made of the large and small branches of trees. The Yaquis lived of course in jacales, but prior to the coming of the padres they had constructed no grandes jacales to serve as temporary churches. Such building was the first thing which Ribas had to organize. After these chapels were set up and while the divine service was being held in them Ribas would see to the construction of larger and permanent fabrics, real churches of which the Yaquis could be as proud on their river as the Suaquis were on theirs.

The next thing would be the baptism of the adults. To facilitate this the pueblos, formerly more numerous and spreading, were reduced to eight. In preparing for adult baptism there was a great deal of encouragement for the missionaries and affairs looked indeed promising. The pagan mothers were proud of their baptized children. They showed them off, played with them with crosses, and were very happy to come with them to Mass and prayers and to the instructions. These pagan mothers would put in an appearance with the offspring, the latter carrying a cross which the mothers had made of sugar cane. They would place the baby on the ground, set up the cross in front of it and thus create spiritual joy and jollity. "Childish actions these," comments Ribas, "which nevertheless brought to us great consolation."[1]

Though it was not in accord with the discipline of the early

[1] Ribas, V, 12.

Church to allow pagans to attend the holy sacrifice of the Mass (this for good reasons during the first centuries) Ribas, in his usual common-sense and right appraisal of circumstances, allowed these mothers to come; otherwise, says he, they might take offense and their own conversion and baptism might be rendered difficult or impossible.

After the grandes jacales had been built therefore and prior to the erection of permanent churches, it behooved Ribas and Basilio to organize for the baptism of the adults. As on the southern river, a course of instruction had to be inaugurated in order that the Indian might have some understanding of the mysteries of the Christian Faith before being admitted through baptism into the organized body of the Church. Thus, so far as his rude untrained mind could comprehend things spiritual and heavenly, the Indian had to be instructed. The fathers would not be without helpers. The faithful Suaquis who had accompanied Ribas were ever at hand to help in the arrangement of the instructions in each pueblo. There would be two each day.

Then, there were a number of youths who had been allowed by their Yaqui parents to attend the school at Sinaloa. These were now well-tutored Christians and they would aid as catechists. Also, the smartest of the Yaqui boys, who with quick memories and better understanding absorbed rapidly the fundamentals, could be used in the instruction even of the adults. This was not uncommon in these missions. It had already been done on the Sinaloa and the Fuerte. Indeed, the parents were often proud to be instructed thus by their sons and they delighted to see them helping and serving at Mass dressed in gown and surplice.[2]

The missionaries began baptisms with the caciques, and this wisely. With the chiefs baptized, their prestige would attract others to follow the example. They were quite willing to receive the holy waters. Several of them were well known to Ribas. They had been leaders in the persuasion of their people many years ago to accept friendship from the Spaniards. Conibomeai was one; Hymaimeai another. After these had been made Christians they became the godparents of all the others in their respective

---

[2]*Ibid.*

pueblos and thus generated a most numerous spiritual progeny. In this way the baptisms ran through all the upper pueblos and when these had been consolidated into the Faith the missionaries went downstream to do the same with the lower and more difficult villages.

The lower river, and especially Tórin, continued to offer the missionaries occasion for exciting and sometimes near tragic experiences, in spite of the fact that the cacique so friendly to the Spaniards had been baptized and given the name of Don Mateo. Here again at Tórin there was another attempt at murder and under the pretext of a sick call. Wiser from the former experience at Tórin, Ribas, who was this time called, took with him some boys and a couple of braves. There was indeed a sick person, a giant of a man. His son, seemingly a sorcerer, was with him. They were both surly. When the father came up to offer his administrations they insulted him, and the son reached for his bow and arrow. Ribas' companions tried to snatch the weapons away, there was a scuffle, and Ribas and the boys made their escape. As they fled an arrow whizzed by them.

Don Mateo when he heard of the outrage acted quickly and strongly. He gathered the people of his pueblo together and apologized for the atrocious insult offered the father. He proposed to make reparation so far as in him lay. One of the boys reported the affair to Hurdaide who sent the lad back with a bundle of arrows to be deposited in the plaza of the pueblo with the message that these arrows would be for the use of the people of Tórin whenever and only when his services demanded it. The arrows remained in the plaza for long and they were never touched.[3]

But not only murder, actual and barbaric butchery took place while Ribas and Basilio were down here baptizing the adults. An Indian girl of the nearby Guayma tribe, attracted by and trusting in the peaceful spirit of Christianity which she heard had come to the Yaquis, had allowed herself to be married to one of the Yaqui tribesmen. It was an insult according to many of the still pagan Yaquis that this girl should contaminate with her

---

[3] *Ibid.*

alien blood the purity of the Yaqui race. Very early one morning
after an all-night revel, heated with drink and dance, a gang of
Yaquis sought out the Guayma woman, dragged her from her
husband and slew her. Then they cut her into bits, placed her
head on the end of a pole and held a fiendish dance with this
morsel of their enemy's body.

Ribas was in a nearby village when all this happened and he
was summoned in haste, for the report had come to him that the
girl was still alive. He arrived too late to save her life, but he had
the courage to break in upon the fiendish revelry and he had
prestige enough to persuade them to desist.[4]

The work went on, nevertheless, without any serious mishap
to the fathers and finally a large part of the tribe on the lower
river as well as on the upper was baptized. After some two years'
labor forty-nine hundred infants and three thousand adults had
been made Christians.[5] While all this was being carried on the
building of the permanent churches in several of the pueblos was
progressing. Each pueblo was organized according to the usual
pattern. Hurdaide appointed a governor and an alcalde for each,
and Ribas named a fiscal and a catechist. The Yaquis became an
organized people and settled down to Christian and civil living.

The change in the Yaqui tribe as the result of this spiritual
development was immense. From wild and warlike they became
tame and peaceful. From wolves and lions, comments Ribas, they
became sheep and lambs. The Yaquis forgot their old-time pride
and laid aside their ancient haughtiness. Polygamy disappeared
and many an old barbaric custom was discontinued. Instead of
roving about to rob and fight, they seemed to enjoy the company
of the fathers, they liked the religious services, they helped about
the sacristy, and they listened to the sermons. They now saluted
with the beautiful Christian words, "Praised be Jesus Christ."
They would walk a distance of five or six miles for Mass on
Sunday. As on the Fuerte River, so also here from time to
time a recently baptized neophyte would come to Ribas and ex-

---

[4]*Ibid.*, V, 14.

[5]*Ibid.* In an early letter to the Provincial Ribas states that at that time
4,000 infants and 900 adults had already been baptized. Cf. *anua* of 1617,
Memorias, pp. 579ff.

press his happiness in his new-found Faith; tell of a peace within him which he had never known before.[6]

The Yaquis' attitude towards their ancient enemies, the Guaymas, north on the coast, and the Nébomes, farther up the river northeast, changed accordingly. The Nébomes understood now that they could pass unmolested through Yaqui territory, and once when the truce was broken by an individual Yaqui the other Yaquis resented it. As for the Guaymas, they received the apology of the murderers of the woman of their nation. These murderers when they became Christians realized the injury they had done and made sincere reparation. The Yaquis made it known that should any of the Guaymas wish to become Christians, they would admit them to their territory and even give them a certain portion of their land for their planting. Numbers of the Guaymas accepted this generous offer in spite of the rather extraordinary number of medicine-men among them who put up a strong opposition.[7]

At Tesamo, however, on the upper river, some Mayos came to Ribas and complained. Whilst they themselves, they averred, had been made to give up all vestiges of their ancient barbarity, the Yaquis were still permitted to keep the scalps they had taken from the Mayos and to hold high revelry with them at night. The Yaqui caciques were called and Ribas asked them to investigate whether this were so. It was indeed true. The chiefs found in some of the houses a goodly number of scalps and other objects of superstition. These were confiscated, a fire was made in the plaza, while every scalp and other barbarous trophy were burned. The Mayos were satisfied.[8]

It was very true, from wolves and lions the Yaquis were become sheep and lambs. They became a loyal and a noble race and never were they so happy or so prosperous as after they had accepted the beneficent doctrines and practices of Christianity. At the end of this same seventeenth century, when that

---

[6]Ribas, V, 13; *anua* of 1617, *Memorias,* pp. 579ff., where the aforementioned letter of Ribas to the Provincial is given.
[7]Ribas, V, 14.
[8]*Ibid.*

parched and arid cactus patch, the peninsula of Lower California, was being organized by Jesuits for missions, it was from the abundance of food and provisions which these faithful Yaquis enjoyed that the missions across the gulf were able to carry on at all. The Yaquis were the Black Robes' greatest consolation; Pérez de Ribas was their first apostle.

CHAPTER XII
MISSION LIFE

As the traveler drives over a modern but dusty road down the right bank of the Yaqui River today, having crossed at Cócorit, he comes after twenty miles to Tórin, the most unruly of all of the eight Yaqui pueblos while Ribas was among them. Both Ribas and Basilio had been threatened there, and there it was later that Basilio was actually shot and wounded with a poisoned arrow. Maybe it is a case of the ancient proverb turned around, and often, thus turned backward, the proverb is as true as in its ordinary form. If the best when corrupted become the worst, the worst when converted and reformed sometimes become the best. This at least was the case with Tórin if we may judge from the visible relics of the mission still surviving. Ribas tells us of a sanctuary or shrine to Our Lady built at Tórin on the brow of a hill which overlooks a beautiful bend in the river.[1] The hill is still there, the river has not changed its course, and a sanctuary built like an enramada still sits upon the summit. The ancient one, no doubt, long ago crumbled away; but the Yaquis are still at Tórin, and they are still devoted to the Christian traditions given them by Ribas.

On the eastern slope of the same eminence is the relic of an ancient church, the unique example in all of the Ribas country of an edifice built solidly of stone. All the other ruins are either of adobe or of brick. Tórin has made amends for its old-time ferocity. But as for other relics or signs of ancient devotion the Yaqui River differs from the Fuerte. On the Yaqui every vestige of the ancient fabrics, except for Tórin, seems to have disappeared.

Here as on the Fuerte there was great and busy activity connected with the permanent church. Ribas repeats, with possible exaggeration, six hundred as the number of savages cooperating in the building of a single structure on the Yaqui. Ribas and Basilio were the architects, the overseers, and even the laborers also. These missionaries chose the workmen, they had the food prepared and brought to the site that the labor be not interrupted. Timbers had to be cut in the hills and carried down. As there

---

[1]V, 19.

were no pack-animals on the Yaqui at this time to carry the beams, the shoulder of the savage bent beneath their weight. When completed these rude fanes in a rude country were beautified and adorned in a rough way with the art and the culture of civilization.

And in this the natives were not only pleased and entertained, they were instructed and refined. If the illiteracy and rudeness of the Middle Ages of Europe were somewhat dispelled by representation of the mysteries of the Faith carved upon the facades of churches or cathedrals, and in beauteous and resplendent tones in colored windows, so here upon the Yaqui River in early modern times the same process of education was carried out. Ribas ordered from Mexico City a large retable for the shrine of Our Lady on the hill at Tórin. He described it and tells us why he had it so. It was a painting of Christ represented as appearing at the final judgment of mankind. The Savior is of benign physiognomy. His mother at His right is being carried in glory to heaven at the hands of angels, reward of her resplendent virtue; while on His left numerous demons are being dashed headlong into hell, punishment of their proud rebellion. This, says Ribas, "in order to impress upon the Indian mind the truths of the Faith."[2]

For beauty and adornment as well as for instruction the fathers procured from the capital tapestries of silk come through the Philippines from China on the galleons that crossed the Pacific and sailed down the coasts of the Californias. On these silken fabrics too were woven the mysteries of the Faith. All this of course cost money, and the fathers procured it by stinting themselves on the yearly salary of three hundred pesos given them by the King of Spain. Most of the missionaries, it seems, thus indulged their self-sacrificing charity. One of Ribas' successors on the Yaqui, Father Juan de Ardeñas, expended in this manner two-thirds of his yearly allowance.[3]

Mass was said every day in the village where Ribas or Basilio happened to be residing. The neophytes were encouraged to attend and many of them did so. On Sundays, however, and on

---

[2]*Ibid.*
[3]Ribas, V, 16.

certain more important feast days, which were more numerous than at present in the United States, attendance at Mass was obligatory. At such time a sermon or instruction would be given to the people. During the period preceding the baptism of the adults, both on the Fuerte and on the Yaqui, instructions in the fundamentals of the Faith were given twice daily, morning and evening, in the pueblos where the fathers happened to be residing. In the other pueblos a *temastián* or catechist conducted these exercises. After the general baptism of the adults, such instructions were held daily for the children, while the adults were encouraged to attend.

Then, on the Yaqui as on the Fuerte, was organized the boys' school and choir. These Indian youngsters were trained to read and to write in Spanish and then to sing and play on musical instruments for the solemnization of the religious services. Thus some of the little Yaquis sang during a solemn Mass, others played on musical instruments, others again served at the altar in gown and surplice. All of this to the delight, of course, of their parents, as Ribas so frequently makes mention. The orchestra, such as Pedro Méndez had formed on the Ocoroni River, was made up of various instruments which Ribas names: the bassoon, the sackbut, the chirimia, and the flute. It is not difficult to realize the elevating and refining influences which were thus allowed to filter into the Yaqui soul through such religious and social exercises as were organized and directed by their missionary Black Robes.

Besides all this, the manner of building their houses was improved, and their villages were laid out in a certain order and symmetry. Each family, besides, was given a plot of ground contiguous to the hut to cultivate and was shown how to do it. Thus truck gardens with their various produce were added to the original native fields of corn, cotton, beans, and squash.

The fiscals had charge of church attendance and in the different villages where Ribas happened to be staying made known those who desired to be married, those who were dangerously ill, those who had been born and needed baptism. They accompanied the padre on his sick calls and on journeys.

The Indian *gobernador* or governor took the place of the Captain with regard to the material order of each village, and there aided him the alcalde and sometimes even a *corregidor* or police officer. As the neophytes regarded the missionary as their real and universal father, they brought to him their petty disputes. He composed their quarrels, he meted out justice and imposed obedience, and the neophytes were perfectly satisfied with whatever the padre would say or do in these petty turmoils. Besides the fiscal, there was often appointed a sacristan whose duty it was to look immediately after the material well-being of the church. In the course of time the houses of the fathers were enlarged so that these Indian officials could meet therein and discuss the affairs of the village together with the father. Soon mules were introduced so that the sowing of crops could be expanded. Later too the fathers would introduce sheep so that wool besides cotton was had for clothing or for barter. This brought about an improvement in their manner of dress. The old-time near-nakedness became among the Yaquis a thing of the past.

As in other districts of these west coast missions Ribas at baptism had these savages shear their long flowing hair of which they had formerly been so proud. The women especially, whose hair often flowed down to their waist, now had it cut to their shoulders. With the men long hair was formerly a sign of valor; now it became a sign of paganism, and it became the fashion to discard the custom.[4]

Polygamy, so rife among the savages, on the Yaqui as well as on the Fuerte, was successfully done away with by the advent of Christianity. We have seen the penance done by the Suaqui chief Anamei on the Fuerte for the rape which he committed shortly after his baptism. On the Yaqui morals had been atrocious. A woman would be the property of one savage for a period, and then pass over to another taking her offspring with her. The facility with which this was done amazed Ribas; but he was consoled to witness the good will with which after baptism the abuse was corrected.[5]

A very important, but negative and disturbing, factor in the

---

[4]Ribas, V, 13.
[5]*Ibid.*

spiritual life of these Yaquis while Ribas was among them was the presence and agitations of the medicine-man or hechicero, sorcerer and wizard, dealer and dabbler in what might be called black magic. Often times these men were converted and baptized and became leaders for right spirituality as they had been before leaders in perverted paganism. Sometimes after conversion the hechicero relapsed. If these men by their signs, their charms, and their incantations got in touch with spirits it should not be surprising. Only a narrow-minded materialism rejects the existence of spirits, and only one thus ultra-conservative can reject the evidence that exists in the annals of the human race that the spirit world can be and has been got in touch with as well among barbarous as among civilized peoples.

True it is that the effects of contact of members of the human race with spirits have been greatly exaggerated, sometimes ridiculously so beyond all rime and reason. Such exaggeration has taken place with regard to reports concerning good spirits with consequent reputed miracles; and also with regard to evil spirits, with the consequent phenomena of fear, terror, and alleged destruction. This exaggeration has led a more scientific and skeptical age into a reaction equally irrational, which has ended in the absolute denial even of the possibility of preternatural or supernatural phenomena. It is indeed difficult for mankind to hold a middle course, his emotions continuing to flow into and to influence his intellectualism. The age in which Pérez de Ribas lived and wrote was particularly uncritical, especially in Latin countries, with regard to alleged supernatural phenomena, and Ribas did not escape this weakness of his age. Like most he was a child of his time, if indeed a somewhat more matured, superior child.

Ribas sometimes accepted too readily and uncritically the occurrence of miracles in the lives of holy men, and this uncritical attitude leads us to suspect him of legend or of exaggeration in some of the phenomena he recounts with regard to the presences and disturbances brought about in his missions, especially the Yaqui mission, in connection with the activities of the hechicero. However, in the case of the Yaquis he was close at hand. This augments but does not complete our confidence.

Ribas lived and wrote during the most atrocious period of the witch superstition, while the work on magic and preternatural phenomena which he read at this time was the Jesuit Martín Antonio Delrío's *Six Books of Inquiring into Magic*. The work, published in Louvain in 1599, became authoritative for the period and went through many editions. Delrío contributed thus to the popular superstition and did his share in prolonging the agonies of the punishment of the alleged crimes of witches.[6] But more of this anon.

It will suffice to relate here one or another case as given by Ribas while he was on the Yaqui. An Indian once told the missionary that over there across the river and among the hills the sorcerers got in touch with evil spirits. An old woman, said the informer, averred that the Devil appeared to her. Ribas says: "The old women testified that the demons would appear to them in the shapes of dogs and cats, coyotes and snakes. . . . Chiefs and fiscals affirmed as a thing well known that these witches went at night to certain dances to which they were invited by the demons and that they flew through the air."[7] Here, of course, the modern reader is provoked to a smile, let us hope not too cynical, for Ribas accepted such tales as true as did most people of this credulous age. But as a matter of plain fact, the hechiceros on the Yaqui, after most of the adults had been baptized, did come within a short distance of stirring up rebellion among the tribe.

The ringleader of this trouble was one who had been converted and who had aided in the conversion of others. But he suffered a relapse and was running deep in his evil ways. The spirit, it was alleged, spoke to him in a loud and strong voice which influenced some who heard it. Then the spirit began visibly to appear. First in the guise of an old man, next day as a youth of twenty. Such a renewal of youth, the spirit said, they too would enjoy would they only leave the fathers and come back to him. The disturbed condition, spreading, became so alarming that Captain

---

[6]Delrío: *Disquisitionum Magicarum Libri Sex in Tres Tomos Partiti,* Louvain, 1599. Other editions appeared in 1601, 1603, 1606, etc. For the encouragement Delrío's work gave to the witch superstition, cf. Lea, *Materials Towards a History of Witchcraft,* II, 640ff.

[7]V, 18.

Hurdaide had to be sent for. He came with a company of soldiers. While he was passing through the first pueblo he was shot at with an arrow. He thought it wise to ignore the incident. Coming to the village where the main trouble was (unnamed by Ribas, but possibly Tórin) Hurdaide demanded of the cacique that the ringleader be delivered up to him.

This was done forthwith. The wizard, when asked why he had been causing this disturbance in the pueblos, replied that the devil had instigated it; that this spirit had appeared to him every day by a poplar tree in the form of a crow; had urged him to kill the fathers, burn the churches, murder the Captain, throw the bells into the river and sweat out or scrape off the oils of baptism. Thus the tribe could get back to its old-time liberty and merry living. Here was evidently a dangerous and seditious character, thought Hurdaide. The Captain had him hanged with two of his fellow conspirators.

Such is an example of what happened from time to time in the missions not only of Pérez de Ribas, but of practically all the other Jesuits who labored among the Indians on either side of the great cordillera. Some of these details have to be discounted, others might well be. Ribas never tells us that he himself heard these voices or actually saw these phenomena. He heard these things from the Indians, but who can deny the exaggerations of a childish and credulous mind. Ribas seems too easily to have given ear to what his neophytes told him. When all is said, the fact remains that these hechiceros, just as they had stirred up the disastrous revolt among the Tepehuanes, so did they in other places either provoke rebellion or cause disquiet and trouble among the neophytes. Such adverse influences were a constant obstacle to the padres; a serious and from the beginning almost a continuous threat to the spiritual life of the newly converted savage.

In spite of all of this and of various other difficulties and temptations which man is heir to, in spite of the periodical inroads of epidemic or deadly plague, which decimated the pueblos and seriously reduced the population, the Yaquis remained strong and numerous as a tribe and steadfast and loyal as a Christian unit. And at the end of this same century, when Salvatierra and Pícolo were opening the permanent missions in the thorny and rock-bound peninsula of Lower California it was these loyal Yaquis, as we have already noted, who from the labor of their hands and the produce of their fields gave the necessary material assistance for the continuation of these poverty-stricken foundations. Ribas had done a magnificent work. His three years among the Yaquis if not the quietest and most peaceful may well have been the most satisfying and the happiest of his life. He left the missions forever in 1620.

CHAPTER XIII

Brilliant Capital of the Americas

Though Pérez de Ribas had been most successful in the mission field, his health had declined seriously; his superiors, moreover, found his capabilities so numerous and varied that they felt they could use him to even greater advantage in administration. One would guess as much even if it had not been indicated two hundred years ago by an old historian of the Jesuit province of New Spain. Francisco Javier Alegre in commenting upon the recall of Ribas from the missions has the following: "Andrés Pérez de Ribas . . . who had been in the missions for sixteen years, was called by obedience to Mexico in order that to his prudence and religious spirit might be confided the most important offices of the Province."[1]

It is impossible for the modern reader to visualize exactly after the lapse of over three hundred years what changes and contrasts city life offered as over against the poverty and privations of the mission. Certain things we can know; others we can only surmise.

From the desolate wilds of the "rim of Christendom" Pérez de Ribas came to live in the most brilliant capital of North America, and he exchanged the rags and squalor of his neophytes for the refined environment of a viceregal court and the seat of a university.

Mexico City as a Spanish capital was a hundred years old the year after Ribas came to reside in it, and the romantic memories of its first decades, as well as the conquest by Hernando Cortés were still fresh in the memories of the older people whose fathers and grandfathers had been among the early pioneers. Mexico City was just as old at that time as a settlement in America of European civilization as San Francisco in California was in the late nineteen-forties. Culturally and historically Mexico City was of vast importance because for a hundred years it had been capital and metropolis of the Americas. There were thirty thousand houses in the capital at this period which might signify a total population including the Indians of close to a hundred thou-

---

[1] II, 123.

sand.[2] Alexander von Humbolt writing almost two hundred years later gives the population of Mexico City in 1804 as between a hundred and thirty-five thousand and a hundred and forty thousand.[3]

The citizens of this capital were made up chiefly of pure Spaniards, creoles, mestizos, and Indians.[4] The Spaniards born in Spain were the leaders and the high officials of the royal government: even the Creoles (of Spanish blood but born in America) were inferior to them, though they could hold minor governmental positions.[5]

---

[2]Priestley, *The Mexican Nation: A History*, p. 140. Alegre citing a letter of the Archbishop Francisco Manso y Zúñiga, to the king in 1630, recounting the havoc wrought by the great flood of that year, says that thirty thousand Indians died and that twenty thousand families were wiped out. Cf. Alegre, II, 181. Though these figures seem exaggerated, they offer some grounds for speculation on the possible population of Mexico City at this period. Thomas Gage, the English Dominican, who was in Mexico City in 1625 says there were resident in the capital between thirty and forty thousand Spaniards. Cf. Lesley Byrd Simpson, *Many Mexicos*, p. 146. Gage may have included Creoles. Priestley, citing no authority, cuts the number of "Spaniards" down to eight thousand. The French Jesuit Taillandier, passing through Mexico in 1708 on his way to India, says that more carriages rolled the streets of Mexico than of any city in France except Paris. There were at that time, the Jesuit avers, 10,000 whites in Mexico City, and although the Spaniards give 200,000 as the total population, he thinks an unprejudiced view would drop the figure to 60,000. Cf. *Lettres Édifiantes et Curieuses Écrites des Missions Étrangères*, t. XI, p. 380 (Paris, 1731). Father Victor Walter writing to his Jesuit superior in 1723 states that the population of the capital was approximated at 300,000. Cf. *Haupstaatarchiv*, Munich, Jesuitica, 294. Transcript in the Bancroft Library, University of California. It is evident no one knew exactly the population of Mexico City.

[3]*Political Essay on the Kingdom of New Spain*, II, 61.

[4]Priestley, *loc. cit.*

[5]There are no figures of this time giving the relative numbers of Spaniards, Creoles, mestizos, and Indians in Mexico City, but there are figures for 1804. For this year Alexander von Humbolt gives 2,500 white Europeans; 65,000 white Creoles; 33,000 Indians; and 10,000 mulattos— 137,000 in all (*op. cit.*, II, 62). However, for the whole of New Spain there are figures for 1805 and again for 1910, which do not help us a great deal for our present purpose. These are as follows for the whole of Mexico: For 1805: Whites 1,000,000 or 18%; Mestizos 2,000,000 or 38%; In-

The viceregal court was splendid indeed, and a glittering aristocracy of Spaniards fluttered about and adorned the viceregal throne. The installation of each new viceroy was a magnificent affair where the Spaniard's love of ceremony and form shone forth at its finest, while the Latin's love of splash and color became manifest to the eye. The entrance of a new viceroy into Mexico City was a play of pageantry which even a northerner of today, not entirely averse to processions and floats, would have gazed upon with entertainment or maybe even with wonder.[6]

Under the viceroy there were the lesser dignitaries of state: the *audiencia* or judges of the royal courts with their president; the head of the royal fisc with his officials of the treasury; the governors of provinces, who on state occasions came into the capital. The ecclesiastical dignitaries—the archbishop, the officers of the inquisition, and the canons of the cathedral—were almost as important and almost as splendid as the officers of state. Indeed, the office of viceroy was not infrequently blended with that of archbishop as in the case of Pedro Moya de Contreras, 1584-1585, who was at one and the same time viceroy, archbishop, and grand inquisitor; and of the Franciscan, Fray García Guerra, 1611-1612, who represented both king and pope.

Surrounding these great personages, especially the secular officials, were the nobility of church and state and the aristocracy of the capital. They made themselves very and colorfully apparent with their gilded coaches-and-four or coaches-and-six in which they lumbered splendidly along the thoroughfares of the city. In the grand public receptions on state occasions, such as the coming of a viceroy or the installation of an archbishop, the nobility formed a frame of color in which stately ceremonies were carried out.

The English Dominican, Thomas Gage, thus describes the capital as he saw it in 1625: "In my time [Mexico City] was thought

---

dians 2,500,000 or 44%. For 1910: Whites 1,500,000 or 7.5%; Mestizos 8,000,000 or 53%; Indians 6,000,000 or 39%. Therefore in that far earlier age of Ribas the percentage of Indians would exceed the percentage of Mestizos and be far greater than that of whites. Cf. Simpson, *The Encomienda in New Spain*, p. 136, note.

[6]Cf. Priestley, *The Coming of the White Man*, pp. 162ff.

to be of between thirty and forty thousand inhabitants, Spaniards, who are so proud and rich that half the city was judged to keep coaches, for it was a most credible report that in Mexico in my time there were above fifteen thousand coaches. It is a by-word that at Mexico there are four things fair, that is to say, the women, the apparel, and the horses, and the streets. But to this I may add the beauty of some of the coaches of the gentry, which do exceed in cost the best of the Court of Madrid and other parts of Christendom; for there they spare no silver, nor gold, nor precious stones, nor cloth of gold, nor the best silks of China to enrich them. And to the gallantry of their horses the pride of some doth add the cost of bridles and shoes of silver.

"The streets of Christendom must not compare with those in breadth and cleanness, but especially in the riches of the shops which do adorn them. Above all, the goldsmiths' shops and works are to be admired. The Indians, and the people of China that have been made Christians and every year come thither, have perfected the Spaniards in that trade. The viceroy that went thither the year 1625 caused a popinjay to be made of silver, gold, and precious stones, with the perfect colour of the popinjay's feathers (a bird bigger than a pheasant), with such exquisite art and perfection, to present unto the King of Spain, that it was prized to be worth in riches and workmanship half a million of ducats. There is in the cloister of the Dominicans a lamp hanging in the church with three hundred branches wrought in silver to hold so many candles, besides a hundred little lamps for oil . . . , every one being made with several workmanship so exquisitely that it is valued to be worth four hundred thousand ducats; and with such-like curious works are many streets made more rich and beautiful from the shops of the goldsmiths. . . .

"Both men and women are excessive in their apparel, using more silks than stuffs and cloth. Precious stones and pearls further much this their vain ostentation; a hat-band and rose made of diamonds in a gentleman's hat is common, and a hat-band of pearls is common in a tradesman; nay a blackamoor or tawny young maid and slave will make hard shift but she will be in fashion with her neckchain and bracelets of pearls, and her ear-bobs of some considerable jewels. . . .

"There are not above fifty churches and chapels, cloisters and nunneries, and parish churches in that city; but those that are there are the fairest that ever my eyes beheld, the roofs and beams being in many of them all daubed with gold, and many altars with sundry marble pillars, and others with brazil-wood stays standing one above another, with tabernacles for several saints richly wrought with golden colours, so that twenty thousand ducats is a common price of many of them. . . ."[7]

Quite a change for Ribas was all of this press of humanity, the glitter of prosperous colonials, and the pomp of official life, from the lonely, often monotonous, and always squalid, conditions of his former existence near the mouth of the Fuerte in Sinaloa or among his Yaquis in the long valleys of Sonora.

As for the Jesuits in Mexico City, they had come only in 1572, fifty-one years after the conquest, and now they had been here for fifty years. They had done very well for themselves and during the whole of Ribas' residence in or near the city until his death they were in a period of development and expansion. Their two large houses, the professed house and the *Colegio Máximo,* apparently enjoyed the highest prestige of any religious communities in the city, the professed house for spiritual ministry and social activity, and the colegio for education. The Jesuits had besides another plant, also educational, called San Ildefonso, organized chiefly for lower Latin studies, and a fourth school, San Gregorio, for Indians.[8]

Before Ribas' arrival in New Spain and then later while he was in the mission field the Jesuit province continued to grow and to expand. After his residence in the capital this growth continued. The total membership of the Jesuit province of New Spain was 107 in 1580; but in 1592 the figure rose to 216, while at the end of the century it had reached 314.[9] When Ribas

---

[7]Quoted in Lesley Byrd Simpson, *Many Mexicos,* pp. 146ff. But over against such splendor of the few must be mentioned the poverty and squalor of the poor Indian and the ragged mestizo. Jesuit missionaries just come from Europe, especially Germans, noted and commented repeatedly in their letters upon these rags.

[8]Jacobsen, *Educational Foundations of the Jesuits in Sixteenth-Century New Spain,* ch. VIII.

[9]Jacobsen, *op. cit.,* p. 152.

returned from the missions the province counted 345 members
of whom 152 were priests, 120 brothers, 46 scholastics (those
engaged in studies), and 27 novices.[10] By 1628 the number had
reached 382.[11] These figures would include those engaged in the
missions of the north, and the growth was effected by those who
came pouring in from Europe and by Creoles and mestizos who
entered the Order from the viceroyalty itself.[12] Colleges were
being started in various cities. One, for instance, in San Luis
Potosí in 1622,[13] one at Puebla in 1625,[14] and in the same year
another at Querétaro.[15]

Ribas, however, resided near but not in the capital immediately
after his return from the missions. For two years he was rector
of the novitiate at Tepotzotlán some twenty-five miles north and
a little west of Mexico City. It looks as if he were sent here for
rest and recuperation, for the official notice in the catalogue of
the province of New Spain for 1620 gives his age as forty-five
and remarks, as we have seen, that his health was weak.[16] We
will recall besides that he was among those permitted the use
of chocolate as is evidenced by a letter in 1622 of Father General
Vitelleschi.[17] Sixteen years in the missions had undermined what
had been a vigorous constitution.[18]

Whether or not health was the cause of Ribas' brief sojourn
in Tepotzotlán, a more restful and salubrious spot in all the valley
of Mexico could hardly have been chosen. For the tranquillity
of his mind as well as for the recuperation of his body this
environment was ideal. Tepotzotlán, still an Indian village and
still bearing upon it with beauty and dignity the ancient buildings
of the novitiate, rests upon the elevated edge of the great valley

[10]*Anua* of 1620, synopsis, *Archiv. S.J. Roman., Mex.* 15, f. 398.
[11]*Anua* of 1628, *loc. cit.,* f. 453.
[12]*Anua* of 1627, *Archiv. Gen. Mis.,* t. 25, f. 185.
[13]*Anua* of 1622, synopsis, *Archiv. S.J. Roman.,* f. 419.
[14]*Anua* of 1625, *loc. cit.,* f. 433.
[15]Ribas, *Corónica,* part II, p. 342, and also the *anua* for that year, *loc. cit.,* f. 436.
[16]*Archiv. S.J. Roman., Mex.* 4, f. 245 v.
[17]Jacobsen, "The Chronicle of Pérez de Ribas," *Mid-America,* XX (Apr. 1938), p. 88.
[18]*Archiv. S.J. Roman., Mex.* 4, f. 153.

of Mexico, while hills lie immediately to the west. The valley
swings up to this chosen site by an easy almost imperceptible
gradation until just near the edge of the Jesuit site the rise becomes perceptible and a plateau is reached. This commands a
wide and sweeping prospect to the east and south which is restful
alike to the eye and to the spirit.

When Ribas arrived its church with graceful facade and
delightful tower had already been built and most of the present
houses of the novitiate had been set up. For the institution had
a founder, the wealthy and pious Don Pedro Ruiz de Ahumada,
kinsman of the celebrated Teresa of Avila.[19] Its most intricately
carved altars, five of them, inlaid with gold, the richest in all of
Mexico, were soon to become the famed ornament of this secluded
fane whose tower rising above the valley can be descried from
miles around. Here, truly, was a spot where Ribas in diminished
health might recuperate his strength in rest and prayer. Here
for two years Ribas would have his residence. He was here in
1620, probably coming early in the year,[20] and he remained until
1622 when he became *socius* or secretary to the Provincial, Father
Juan Lorencio.[21]

Supposing then that Ribas enjoyed a capable minister to attend
to the temporal ordering of the house and farm, and was assured
that the novices were well taken care of by their master, we can
conclude that Ribas could really relax from his labors as missionary and regain his diminished physical powers. We can only
suppose that this was the happy development, for there is no
record of the situation. Be that as it may, in two years he was
assigned to more active and important work in the capital.

He left the seclusion of Tepotzotlán in 1622 and went definitely
to reside in the heart of Mexico City. This was his residence
for the rest of his long and busy life, excepting a period spent
on official business in Europe and brief absences from the capital
in connection with his various duties as secretary to the provincial and later as provincial himself.

---

[19]Valle, *El Convento de Tepotzotlán*, p. 16.
[20]*Archiv. S.J. Roman., Mex.* 4, f. 245 v.
[21]Alegre, II, 152.

The two main houses of the Jesuits in Mexico City at this time and indeed until the expulsion a century and a half later were, as we have said, the Colegio Máximo, or Great College, and a residence for priests engaged in the ministry, called the *casa profesa* or professed house. Ribas resided in the latter. This year of 1622 it numbered twenty-three priests and twenty-two brothers, including the Provincial, whose official residence it was, with two secretaries, one of whom was Ribas, the other a brother; also the procurator of the province with a brother assistant or companion.[22]

The professed house was formally opened on February 3, 1592, when four fathers and one brother came to live in a very unfit house on property which had been donated in 1584 by Hernando Nuñez de Obregón, a near relative of the Jesuit Father Pedro Mercado. Though permission for this residence was granted in all due form both by the Viceroy and the Archbishop, an appeal in the courts against it was started by three religious orders who had houses close by. The case was bandied about from one jurisdiction to another, while both parties sent procurators to Rome to win their case in a last appeal. Finally in 1595 the question was settled in favor of the Jesuits.

In the meantime the four fathers in their shabby quarters and tiny church, which was in fact only the vestibule of the house, conciliated even their adversaries by their friendly and unobtrusive demeanor and by the energetic ability of their spiritual ministrations. The Jesuits were within their rights and had foreseen success, for in 1594 Dr. Pedro Sánchez was sent especially from Rome to be superior of the house "in order," as Alegre says, "that the head of the province might imbibe the true spirit of the Society from the same central fountain from which it has always so successfully flowed."[23] So soon as the suit was settled the construction of a new and suitable dwelling and a church was begun, supported partly from a sum of fifty thousand

---

[22]*Anua* of 1622, *Archiv. S.J. Roman., Mex.* 15, f. 107; cf. also *anua* of 1625, *Archiv. Gen. Mis.,* t. 25, f. 124. In the professed house lived "professed fathers", namely, those priests who took the solemn vows. Such houses were abolished after the suppression of the Society in 1773.

[23]Alegre, I, 272f.

pesos left for that purpose by the royal treasurer, Juan Luis de Ribera.[24]

This professed house became the center of the administration of the affairs of the province of New Spain. We have the record. Its numbers increased down through the years until in Ribas' time, thirty years after its beginning, it housed, as we have said, twenty-three fathers and twenty-two brothers. In 1624 this community numbered twenty fathers and sixteen brothers,[25] the same in 1625 less four brothers,[26] and the same in 1628.[27] Ribas came to reside amidst a respectable community of forty odd, less by almost half, it is true, than the number of Jesuits in the Colegio Máximo.

The Jesuits were very proud of the success of the spiritual ministrations of this professed house. The *anua* of 1622, speaking of the *domus profesa*, has the following: "Our professed house of Mexico seems to be not dissimilar to a living tree planted in the midst of the garden of Paradise. For it is set in the very core and center of the city and generously dispenses its spiritual pabulum. What estimate, therefore, the townspeople have of us is well illustrated by the crowds, both of the nobility and of the people, which all the year through frequent our church. These gladly accept the administration of the fathers and frequently receive the sacraments to the rich profit of their souls."[28] Interesting enough, this same figure of speech is carried on through various reports of following years.[29]

The anua says well that the professed house was physically in the very heart of the town. Rising only two blocks west of the plaza, the *zócalo*, fronting the cathedral, and almost in the shadow of the magnificent fabric, the professed house was engulfed by the busy life of the metropolis which swirled around it all day long. Nor was it far from the intellectual center of

---

[24]*Loc. cit.*, p. 248.

[25]*Anua* of 1624, *Archiv. S.J. Roman.*, f. 121.

[26]*Anua* of 1625, *loc. cit.*, f. 131.

[27]*Anua* of 1628, *loc. cit.*, f. 140.

[28]*Anua* of 1622, *Archiv. S.J. Roman., Mex.* 15, f. 107; *Archiv. Gen. Mis.*, t. 25, p. 2, Spanish text of same.

[29]Cf. *anuas* of 1624, 1625, 1628, *Archiv. S.J. Roman., Mex.* 15, ff. 122, 132, 140.

the city, the Colegio Máximo. A walk from the college of what English-speaking Americans would call three blocks south and then four blocks west, passing between the plaza and the cathedral, would bring Ribas in ten minutes to his new home.[30] Such a deep mark did this Jesuit spiritual center of the professed house and the church make upon the capital of Mexico that the old names still apply, and one will see designated on modern maps in Spanish the "Casa Profesa" and in English the "Profesa Church"! In the mid-twentieth century the old fane had begun to lean and money was being collected for its preservation.

His new position would have pleased Ribas even if obedience had not ordered him thither. He was coming to a well-regulated and busy Jesuit community. "Domestic discipline flourishes," says one report, "all make the spiritual exercises every year where in this holy leisure freed from distractions and the various works of soul-saving and aiding the neighbor, the fathers recuperate their strength. Thus revived and fortified they are able with greater fruit to go to hospitals, call on the sick, aid the dying, visit prisons, console criminals, snatch souls from sin and moral danger, abolish evil habits, compose peace, introduce good customs, preach often, be assiduous in hearing confessions, in one word, be occupied in such holy works as the Society all over the world . . . performs with such resounding success."[31] Thus does a seventeenth-century provincial of New Spain, Juan Laurencio, expatiate with enthusiasm in his report to the General at Rome upon the works which his Jesuits were carrying on. This enthusiasm will not seem exaggerated when one finds it recorded that during the Lent of the following year, 1623, the fathers of this house preached one hundred and forty sermons.[32]

Ribas here would witness and be part of the organization of numerous activities, festive and otherwise. Signs of development and progress were frequent. Shortly before Ribas came, an elegant tabernacle had been installed in the church, "resplendent with gold and shining with silver." This ornament lent an added richness to the Mardi Gras devotions of 1622, organized each

---

[30]Cf. Jacobsen, *op. cit.*, p. 82, map.
[31]*Anua* of 1622, *Archiv. S.J. Roman., Mex.* 15, f. 108.
[32]*Anua* of 1623, *Archiv. Gen. Mis.*, t. 25, f. 76.

year to act as a counterpoise to the secular celebrations of the capital. These services were and still are referred to as the Forty Hours' Devotion. The altar and sanctuary, elaborately decorated for the occasion with candles and tapestries and flowers, was a point of pride with the Jesuits of Mexico City. This offered a fit setting for the rites of Mass and Benediction, and all the city, so it appears from the contemporary reports, turned out to attend one or another of the services.

The first day of the Forty Hours' Devotion of 1622, the viceroy and his ministers graced the morning service together with the Knights of the Order of Santiago; the second day the officials of the Inquisition attended in their robes of office. But on the third and closing day the Archbishop of Mexico himself, Juan Pérez de la Serna, with his suite brought dignity and color to the service.[33] The fathers at this time were overwhelmed with work and were unable to supply all the demands made upon them for the hearing of confessions. Great crowds moved up to the high altar each morning for Holy Communion. Thus the spiritual Mardi Gras of 1622; thus the activity and the prestige of the casa profesa at the beginning of Ribas' residence there.

However, such a celebration was a yearly procedure, with the Viceroy and all the rest of it. While the secular public ran to amusement, the spiritual element prayed in the churches. In 1627 a golden eagle adorned the altar for these celebrations, while gems and diamonds of the Viceroy's wife glittered about the monstrance at Benediction. Five hundred candles in silver candelabra artistically placed added light and warmth to the universal splendor.[34]

In January, 1624, occurred the notorious riots in the city occasioned by the populace taking sides in a famous quarrel which broke out between the Viceroy, the Marqués de Gelves, and the Archbishop, Juan Pérez de la Serna. It was the old story of an overlapping of jurisdictions, the spiritual and the secular. The people took the side of the Archbishop and ran amuck with the civilian guards of the Viceroy. Stones and brickbats were hurled

---

[33]*Anua* of 1622, *Archiv. S.J. Roman., Mex.* 15, f. 108.

[34]Cf. for example the *anua* of 1626, *Archiv. Gen. Mis.*, t. 25, f. 152; *anua* of 1627, *loc. cit.*, f. 188, etc.

by the mob; arquebuses of the Viceroy's guard spoke in reply and scattered death. Heads were broken and blood flowed. The main plaza before the cathedral then in construction was the focal center of these disturbances. Jesuits from the professed house, which was only two blocks west, mingled with the rioters to try to quiet the trouble and to administer to those who had been hurt. One of the padres went down in the fracas but was not killed.[35]

It was not long after this that a Dutch ship put in at Vera Cruz. But the officers did not land the vessel. They were perhaps fearful of the Inquisition, for the ship carried heretics; or perhaps they feared the rigid regulations on foreign trade now long existent. The sailors, however, deserted. Some swam ashore, others came in rowboats. They were forthwith arrested, hustled to Mexico City and flung into the prisons of the Inquisition. One of the fathers of the professed house was versed in the Low German dialect spoken by the Dutch, and he was happy to go to the prison to ease the discomfort of these poor fellows. Still more eager was the padre to convert such unfortunate heretics to the true Faith.[36]

Nothing, perhaps, during Ribas' residence in the casa profesa surpassed in splendor the celebration of the occasion of the beatification of Saint Francis Borgia. Grand things had taken place, it is true, the previous year, when both Ignatius Loyola and Francis Xavier were canonized, at which time also Aloysius Gonzaga was declared blessed. But Borgia's celebration of 1624, judging from the reports, surpassed anything the city had ever seen before.

On the morning of the great day every dignitary, lay and clerical, of the capital and the communities of every religious order turned out for Mass at the church of the professed house. The Viceroy, with wife and daughter, the Vicar of the Archbishop (the dignitary himself must have been ill or absent), the officers

---

[35]*Anua* of 1624, *Archiv. Gen. Mis.,* t. 25, f. 77; Alegre, II, 146. For an extended account of these picturesque and exciting riots see Bancroft, *History of Mexico,* III, chapters 2 and 3, and Rivera, *Los Gobernantes de México,* I, 114 ff.

[36]*Anua* of 1624, *Archiv. S.J. Roman., Mex.* 15, f. 122.

of the Inquisition, the Knights of Santiago, and the various religious orders were all present for Solemn Mass. But the chief color and wildest fling of the celebration was after sundown when a procession was organized some distance from the church and moved noisily towards it for solemn benediction. Viceroy and officials, archbishop's vicar, and clerics with the religious orders were again present. The Viceroy's suite was ablaze with torchlight, torches lit up the dignitaries and religious in his wake. There was a band, there was singing; there were confetti and festoons; and as the procession entered the church a volley of artillery boomed from the guns of the fort.

The services over, the celebrations continued late into the night. The blare of harsh trumpets which at intervals broke over the city were relayed with the softer call of horns and cornets. Colored lights and fireworks of various description lent flash and color to the streets, and the Roman candle, as the Latin text says, spouting intermittently a ball of fire amid a shower of sparks, variegated the exciting activities.[37] The populace were regaled also by spinning wheels which in whirling flame and color with a scattering of sparks made gorgeous designs in fire. Even the three Jesuit houses of the city were ablaze with lights which were kept burning far into the night. Ribas, we fear, kept late hours this festive occasion, and knowing him from the missions we think he had joy and jollity with the rest.[38]

It would be a mistake, however, to think that Ribas resided continuously in the capital. His duties as secretary to the provincial would take him to the various Jesuit houses and colleges which extended from Guatamala south to Zacatecas north, and from Vera Cruz to Guadalajara. When Provincial Juan Laurencio visited the newly founded college at San Luis Potosí in 1622 Ribas was probably with him. And as there were in all during the sixteen-twenties twenty-one houses of the Society, fourteen

---

[37]Nothing else but the Roman candle is indicated by the following description in Latin: *missilia pulveris tormentarii papyraciis inclusi tuberulis jacula deeminebant in aera, ubi fluminis imitata stridorem, dum jam jam evanescerent stellulas emittebant et crepitum.—Ibid.*

[38]*Anua* of 1624, *loc. cit.;* cf. also *Archiv. Gen. Mis.,* t. 25, ff. 100 ff., for Spanish text of *anua.*

of them being colleges, Ribas, if he accompanied the Provincial, was often absent from the city.[39] In 1626 Father Diego de Sosa was sent out from Rome to be visitor to the whole province. Ribas now became secretary to him also.[40] It seems rather certain that at least during this year Ribas made the rounds of all the houses with the official visitor from Rome. Perhaps he longed to visit the missions, but provincials and provincial visitors usually did not make this long and difficult journey; they appointed a Visitor to act with delegated authority.

Thus were the first years of Ribas in the capital taken up in circumstances and with activities in utter contrast to his sometimes dangerous, sometimes quiet and placid, life in the missions. Evidently he had given satisfaction as a religious man and as an administrator, for this same year of 1626 the rectorship of the Colegio Máximo was imposed upon him. He became now superior himself, seldom thereafter to doff the robe of authority.

---

[39]*Anua* of 1628, *Archiv. S.J. Roman., Mex.* 15, f. 140.

[40]*Synopsis Soc. Jesu,* col. 555. Astrain, V, 313, note 3, who mentions this, gives the seemingly mistaken date of 1629.

CHAPTER XIV

COLLEGE PRESIDENT

From secretary to Juan de Laurencio, the provincial of New Spain, Ribas became secretary to the official Visitor sent out from Rome, Diego de Sosa. From this he stepped up to the place of college president and rector of the largest Jesuit community in Mexico.[1] Pérez de Ribas became rector of the Colegio Máximo in 1626, the very year of Sosa's visitation and it looks as if the appointment came from the Visitor himself, who could have been thus empowered by the General Vitelleschi. Ribas fulfilled two terms of three years each as rector, quite a common occurrence. The next record we have of him makes the padre *praepositus* or superior of the casa profesa, and this in 1632.[2]

The Colegio Máximo, literally "Greatest College," enjoyed as its full and official title *Colegio Máximo de San Pedro y San Pablo,* because it was named after the two apostles, Peter and Paul. The term "Máximo" was official to the Jesuit Order, designating a college attended by Jesuit scholastics or students in order that they receive the formation in philosophy and theology which the Order wished to give them. Technically such a college was the most important which each province of the Order could possess; the other colleges dedicated to the education of secular youth were considered of less degree. Each province was supposed to have such a seminary for the training of its young men.

But this institution in Mexico City, which soon outshone in activity and local importance the old University of Mexico, was a combination of both types. It was ecclesiastical seminary and secular college combined. It was a seminary both for young Jesuits and clerics from out the Order, and a college for the secular youths of the city. On its religious side it represented a rather large community of Jesuits living together under the rule of their Order.[3] The college had been founded not many years before by Father Pedro Sánchez, the learned doctor and former professor at the University of Alcalá in Spain. Appointed superior

---

[1]*Archiv. S.J. Roman., Mex.* 4, f. 268 v.
[2]*Ibid.,* f. 294 v.
[3]Jacobsen, *Educational Foundations of the Jesuits,* ch. IX and X.

of the group destined for Mexico in 1572, he led the initial band of fourteen Jesuits across the Atlantic.

Pedro Sánchez established several smaller schools before he saw his way clear, financially, to set about the building of what was to become the Jesuit center of the capital. But in 1576 the rich owner of the mines of Ixmiquilpán, Alonso de Villaseca, who had been so generous to the fathers from the start, came forward again with a magnificent gift of 150,000 pesos. Father Sánchez could now proceed with that which had been his aim since his arrival in the New World, the building and organization of a Jesuit center which would be called the *Colegio Máximo de San Pedro y San Pablo*.

Center indeed it was, especially in its early years. The full course of training, spiritual and intellectual, for young Jesuits, covering many years, proceeded within its walls, from the two years' spirituality of the novitiate, through letters, philosophy, and theology, to the final touching-off process of the tertianship, which was an added year of straight spirituality. Non-Jesuit clerics attended some of these courses. Then it was a college for the secondary and higher education of young Spaniards of the capital, being high school, college and university combined. Within a few years of its foundation it was tutoring seven hundred students. It housed all the Jesuit professors of the institution and the teachers of the smaller schools located nearby, called San Gregorio and San Ildefonso. Besides it was the residence of others: visitors, the sick or retired, and those priests who were engaged in the spiritual ministrations of the city. Later, when other houses were built to carry on some of this work, its Jesuit community diminished.[4]

When in 1626 Pérez de Ribas became the head of this educational center it was just half a century old. Ribas was just in time to celebrate its golden jubilee. Its religious community had diminished, for the professed house had taken from it those engaged in spiritual ministrations, and the novitiate in Tepotzotlán had taken away the novices. And in this same year of 1626 some of the young Jesuits began to do their studies in the college

---

[4]Jacobsen, *loc. cit.;* Astrain, III, 131ff.

of *Santo Espíritu* in Puebla. But as far as general work and activity, education and otherwise, were concerned, the Colegio Máximo partook of the general progress of the whole Jesuit province.[5]

"The first fifty years" had been splendid; the next fifty would be equally so. If shortly after its inception the college numbered seven hundred students, the figure had risen to eight hundred, with sixty graduates, in 1622 when Ribas came to the capital to live.[6] Three years later, and one before Ribas' presidency, the figures show nine hundred students with one hundred graduates.[7] This was quite a natural growth, for the population of the city was likewise increasing during these years.[8] Near the Colegio Máximo was the royal college of San Ildefonso and the seminary for Indians, San Gregorio;[9] nearby too were the buildings of the old University of Mexico founded by Charles V, in 1551.[10]

Ribas therefore as rector of the Colegio Máximo was in the center of humanism and of intellectual culture of the Americas. The only rival to Mexico was Lima in Peru. But both because of its youth and of its greater distance from the mother country, Lima was outshone by the capital of New Spain. As for the rest of North America at this time, culturally it was non-existent. Our date of 1626, the very year Thomas Gage was in town and described the city, was only nineteen years after the beginning of the infant English colony at Jamestown and only six years since the Pilgrim Fathers had landed on Plymouth Rock. Harvard College, oldest school of higher learning in the United States, was founded ten years after Ribas became president of a well-organized, thriving college. As for the next oldest schools of the English colonies, William and Mary, and Yale, they did not make an appearance until decades later. Yet, history's record shows that these latter enjoyed eventually a greater continuity.

At the coming of the Jesuits in 1572 a humanistic and cultural

---

[5]*Anua* of 1627, *Archiv. Gen. Mis.*, t. 25, f. 185.
[6]*Anua* of 1622, *Archiv. S.J. Roman., Mex.* 15, f. 108.
[7]*Anua* of 1625, *loc. cit.*, f. 132.
[8]*Anua* of 1627, *loc. cit.*, f. 185.
[9]*Anuas, passim*, and Jacobsen, *op. cit.*, ch. VIII.
[10]Jacobsen, *op. cit.*, p. 82, map.

tradition had already been set in Mexico; but the Jesuit educators organized and advanced the tradition. The printing press had been introduced as early as 1535 or 1536 and print-shops maintained themselves from that time continuously in Mexico City. Writings—historical, literary, and devotional—soon appeared and of these a few of the historical works are still living. The ancient classics, the works of Homer, Cicero, Virgil, Plutarch, and the rest, circulated freely.[11]

But although the University of Mexico founded by Charles V in 1551 had been holding classes since 1553, nineteen years before the Jesuits came, its interests were chiefly philosophical and theological, while literary humanism according to the best standards of the Renaissance had to await in Mexico, as it did in the capitals of Europe, the coming of the Jesuits to receive its systematized organization.[12] They took Christian humanism as activated in the schools of the Brethren of the Common Life and at the College of Montaigue in Paris and graded it with the courses of philosophy and theology so that it all formed an organized whole. The *ratio studiorum,* which received its final form in 1599, crystallized this organization.[13] When, therefore, Ribas became college president his Colegio Máximo enjoyed the most enlightened educational system of the age and had progressed under it to become the acknowledged intellectual leader of New Spain. Reflection of confidence and satisfaction in this achievement is a passage from the annual letters where the college is referred to as "the unique center and emporium of learning for the whole kingdom to which for the sake of acquiring knowledge multitudes of the young flock from the remotest corners of the viceroyalty."[14]

Thus into what we call now in the United States secondary schools and junior colleges the finest spirit and culture of the Renaissance was introduced by the Jesuits. In Mexico City the pioneers in this work for the youth of New Spain were Fathers

---

[11]Priestley, *The Coming of the White Man,* pp. 145ff.

[12]In Europe the Oratorians and Capuchins were also progressive in this field of education. Cf. Janelle, *The Catholic Reformation,* ch. VII.

[13]Farrell, *The Jesuit Code of Liberal Education,* ch. I-III.

[14]*Anua* of 1624, *loc. cit.,* f. 122.

Juan Sánchez Vaquero, Pedro Mercado, and Vicente Lanuchi. These taught the classics in the Colegio Máximo before the opening of the seventeenth century.[15] When Ribas became rector, therefore, he enjoyed the fruit of a mature tradition. He saw issuing from the halls of his college on set occasions—feasts of the Church, a reception of the Viceroy, or the opening of the scholastic year—oratory (sometimes windy and fulsome it is true), and verse (sometimes empty and halting be it said), which flowed from the pens and the voices of the undergraduates. The rector, Pérez de Ribas, just now passing middle age, could well be the intelligent inspiration of all of it and he could look benignly upon the callow successes of the youthful efforts.

As with the professed house, so with the Colegio Máximo: its halls and its church were honored from time to time by the presence of the Viceroy and his suite. More particularly was this the case between 1624 and 1635, during the incumbency of Rodrigo Pacheco y Osorio, Marqués de Cerralvo, because he was, above the other Viceroys of his period, more intimate with the fathers. The Marqués honored the college on Ascension Day, for instance, in 1624, while Ribas was still at the professed house.

The dignitary came with his wife and his chaplain and with other officials of his court. As this was the year of Cerralvo's inauguration the wife of the outgoing Viceroy, the Marqués de Gelves, was still in the capital, and it was a mark of the friendliness of the occasion that the marquesa made up the official party. Indeed, during the Solemn Mass in the college which began the celebration, the two ladies received Holy Communion, while the sermon was delivered by the official chaplain. After entertainments of various kinds, material, spiritual, and intellectual, which probably consumed the greater part of the day, it was time for the Viceroy to leave. This was done with no little éclat. Preceded by the students and the college orchestra he was accompanied in state to the vice-regal palace which lay a short distance south hard by the great cathedral.[16] Grateful for such return of friendship, the Viceroy in 1628 had the street leading to the college

---

[15]Jacobsen, op. cit., p. 118.
[16]Anua of 1624, Archiv. S.J. Roman., Mex. 15, f. 123.

paved with stone and as the district covered lower ground, he had an effective drainage system installed.[17]

Such fêtes and celebrations had now for long been frequent in the capital. The festivities were most always accompanied by the staging of plays—comedies, tragedies or mere pageants—by the scholars of Colegio Máximo. As early as 1574, when the Jesuits were only two years old in Mexico, the Jesuits' boys celebrated the titular feast of their college, Peter and Paul, by a tragicomedy in honor of the apostles. The following year the Viceroy and the nobles of the capital witnessed a like performance. And so this European Jesuit tradition of drama for the culture of their students went on in the New World year after year in the capital as in other centers where Jesuit colleges existed.[18]

In 1578, for instance, All Saints' Day was celebrated by a festival lasting a whole octave. The minor Jesuit schools participated. A procession was organized in which more than two hundred students rode on horseback along the line of march which was adorned with eight triumphal arches displaying elaborate figures symbolic of the virtues and merits of the saints. In this brilliant pageant Indians marched "carrying crosses, banners, and images placed on more than two hundred gilded litters." Then came the sodalities with their standards, Jesuits clad in surplice, and finally the Viceroy, Don Martín Enríques de Almanza, with his official family. As the parade halted, youths dressed as saints or angels read poetry, declaimed, and performed pantomine. The streets were aflame with silks of various colors, with canopies and pictures and shields enscribed with verse. The Jesuit church was exquisitely decorated and the windows of the homes were set off with ingenious trimmings. "Kettledrums, trumpets and rustic instruments furnished the music" while *"cascarmes* containing perfumed water filled the air with fragrance." Masses and prayers, dances and fireworks, implemented this round of festivities to completion.

On this occasion a drama, which became a classic, was staged by the pupils. *Triunfo de los Santos* was its title and for decades,

---

[17]*Anua* of 1628, *loc. cit.,* f. 142.
[18]Johnson, *An Edition of "Triunfo de los Santos",* ch. II.

like the Passion Play of Santa Clara in California, it was staged and restaged for the benefit of students and public alike.[19]

The tradition of literary and artistic splendor thus early set by the students of the Colegio Máximo continued on and was still in full flower during Ribas' incumbency as rector of the institution. In June 1610 the Jesuits held a mammoth celebration to commemorate the beatification of their founder, Ignatius Loyola; in 1620 again there were "masks, fireworks, music, bull-fights, processions, sermons" to welcome the news of St. Francis Xavier's beatification; we have already described the festivities in honor of St. Francis Borgia in 1624 when Ribas was resident in the professed house. Another celebration in Borgia's honor seems to have taken place the following year when, as had been done before, the municipal council of Mexico City aided the fathers in the liquidation of the expenses for the show. During such occasions the students of the colegio engaged habitually in plays, pageants, pantomimes, mock battles and in expositions of their literary talents.[20]

By 1646 the Jesuit college possessed an auditorium with seats on a double level. The stage was adorned with images and a *cathedra* made of precious woods. Here the literary contests and the dramatic pieces were henceforth performed. Ribas lived to witness such prosperity and, as is the wont of humans, probably referred occasionally to his own years as rector, "the old days," when such facilities were not enjoyed.

Lent and Advent were always times of more than ordinary activity in the capital, both with the Colegio Máximo and the professed house. The young Jesuits who were students at the college went out on Thursdays and Saturdays during these seasons to offer spiritual instruction in various parts of the city, especially in the poorer sections. In such districts, amidst the dirty and dingy factories for woolen fabrics, these Jesuit students sought out the poorest of the poor of every color that lived in

---

[19]We have all of these details from the famous *Carta del Padre Pedro de Morales,* who under date of February 22, 1579, sent a minute and colorful narrative of the events to Father General, Everard Mercurian. Cf. Johnson, *op. cit.,* pp. 11ff.

[20]*Ibid.,* p. 29.

Mexico—white, red, and black.[21] For even at this early date there was in the capital, besides the ever-present and multitudinous Indian, a goodly addition of Negro blood, pure and mixed.

Some of the fathers even preached to these Negroes in their own language. And the Negro was true to form and color. As Livingstone in the nineteenth century noted on the banks of the Zambesi, as the twentieth-century Jesuit has experienced in Belgian Congo, and as the American public likewise knows full well, so did these seventeenth-century Jesuits of New Spain remark and put into the record. "These people," says the anua of 1624, "are easily bent toward piety and thereafter firmly adhere to it."[22] And we read here of their cheerful tempers.

On certain occasions during Lent and Advent the younger students of the college and of the other Jesuit schools went in procession arranged in organized sections from the Jesuit center through the crowded streets of the city to the church of the professed house. They chanted hymns and the catechism as they marched along preceded by a large crucifix held aloft by a student. Come before the church they would pause, group themselves before the entrance, and listen to a spiritual exhortation fitted to their youth. The townspeople gathered about to witness and be edified at the sight.[23]

There were two fraternities in the college of a spiritual character, called sodalities. These were under the patronage of and were dedicated to Mary, the mother of God. One was for the younger students, the other for their seniors. These were the lads who took the lead in the spiritual activities we have mentioned. Feast days of the Blessed Virgin, such as her nativity or assumption into Heaven, were marked for especial activity and devotion. Solemn Mass was followed by literary exercises, poems and orations on the quality and virtues of the mother of God. Following an age-old custom in the Church, each Saturday was distinguished by activities in her honor: Mass in the morning and in the evening a musical concert.[24]

---

[21]*Anua* of 1628, *loc. cit.,* f. 141.
[22]*Loc. cit.,* f. 123.
[23]*Anua* of 1624, *loc. cit.,* f. 122.
[24]*Anua* of 1625, *loc. cit.,* f. 132.

Of all of this Father Pérez de Ribas while he was rector of the college was the head and the heart. He would be either the direct initiator of such functions as Solemn Mass before the Viceroy and his court or he would be consulted previously as to their advisability by such officials as the prefect of studies or the senior from among the professors. These today we would refer to as dean or the head of a department.

Every college president who is a Jesuit, being thus rector of the religious community, holds the supreme domestic jurisdiction over the men of his community. The rector carries thus upon his shoulders responsibility for the discipline of the house and in a general manner for its spiritual direction. In these duties the rector is aided by subordinate officials who derive their authority from him.[25] During his first year of office, for instance, Ribas had under his spiritual authority twenty-three fathers, nineteen scholastics (young Jesuits not yet ordained), and twenty-seven temporal coadjutors or brothers. These latter attended to the material necessities and orderliness of the institution. Of the priests, three this year were professors of theology, three of philosophy, and four, with one scholastic, taught grammar and rhetoric.[26]

Such was the spiritual family of Ribas. To be a good religious superior he must be real father, not only to the scholastics and brothers, but also to the other priests of the community, even though some be older than himself. In such spiritual relationships age does not count. We enjoy no distinct reports concerning Ribas' comportment during these years at the Jesuit center. But if through intelligence and kindness he was so able to win the respect and affection of the redskin of the wilds of Sinaloa and Sonora, the presumption is that he succeeded equally well or even better with the Black Robe of the city. This presumption meets practically complete confirmation in this, that given one post

---

[25]Constitutiones Societatis Jesu, pars. IV, cap. X.

[26]Anua of 1626, Archiv. Gen. Mis., t. 25, f. 175. From this anua it appears that there were some novices living in the capital at this time. Ribas may have had some authority over them. This may be why in the official record (Mex. 4, 268 v.) he is mentioned as master of novices as well as rector.

of authority, he mounted ever higher until he stood at the summit of whatever authority headquarters at Rome could confer upon him (though it does not always happen that those promoted are fit for the office).

Ribas may have engaged to his consolation in certain works of the ministry which would be a relief to his administrative duties. In 1625, for instance, the rector of the Colegio preached in the parish church called *Diva Chateriana* and in the hospital of the Immaculate Conception, while every Sunday evening he delivered in the college church an historical lecture on certain phases of the lives of the saints.[27] Ribas probably consoled himself for the cares of office by engaging in such ministry, and he may or may not have had a confessional in the church.

We cannot close this chapter on Ribas' rectorship without mentioning a heavy trial which came upon him together with all the residents of the city. It was the great flood of 1629 and 1630.[28]

When we remember that Tenochtitlán, the Aztec name for Mexico City, was built upon the waters of a great lagoon which spread hundreds of square miles over the valley of Mexico it can be appreciated that the city rested upon lower ground. Gradually after the conquest the lagoon shriveled and shrank until after a hundred years of European enterprise, what with drainage, what with dykes and bulkheads, what with a distribution of the waters for the irrigation of the fields of the valley, the capital was finally drained of its water, but remained always near the edge of the lagoon. In time of extraordinary precipitation the waters would rise and spread and there would be danger of flood to the city. This is exactly what happened at the end of the sixteen-twenties, one hundred and ten years after Cortés and the conquest.

There had been some heavy rains in 1627. That year the Río

---

[27]*Anua* of 1625, *loc. cit.*, f. 132.

[28]Both Alegre, II, pp. 178ff. and the *anua* of 1629-1630, *Archiv. Gen. Mis.*, t. 25, 216ff. give detailed accounts of this dire calamity. Alegre draws from the *anua*. Cf. also Cavo, *Los Tres Siglos de Méjico*, lib. VII, pp. 88ff.; Rivera, *Los Gobernantes de México*, I, 118ff.; and Bancroft, III, 86ff.

Cuautitlán burst its banks and poured its waters into the lagoons of Zumpango and Cristóbal and into the great *Laguna de México*. The giant pools rose and spread putting parts of the capital under water. In this emergency Viceroy Cerralvo, called upon the Provincial, Gerónimo Díez, for some fathers to aid in the direction of the necessary works to strengthen and heighten the retaining walls of the dykes and ditches. These had been built according to plans drawn by the engineer Boot to restrain and divert the flooding waters of the streams which tumbled down from the mountains and of the lagoons which rose and swelled on the fringe of the city.[29]

Six Jesuits engaged in the work to the satisfaction of all: two fathers, Christóbal Angel and Bartolomé Santos, and four brothers. The two fathers had already in 1607 during a similar danger been an aid to the then Viceroy, Luis de Velasco, Marqués de Salinas. And now in 1627 their work was done and the people were satisfied and grateful for Jesuit aid even in things material and scientific. Preparations for still further works were being made when calamity visited the city.

The year 1628 was dry; but during the rainy season of 1629, extending into the spring of 1630, the continuous rains surpassed anything which the oldest residents of the city remembered to have witnessed. The dykes which had been restored with such care and labor to circumscribe and restrain the waters of the lagoons, made only of adobe, broke and let in the waters to run over the capital; the streams tumbling from the mountains which frame the city overflowed their banks so that other parts of the valley of Mexico began to suffer. Extraordinary havoc was wrought by the flooding waters of the Río Aculhuacán. Already by September 5 the lower districts of the capital were under water, and canoes were paddled through the streets. But on the morning of the twenty-second, the whole city woke up to find itself submerged after a most extraordinary downpour of thirty-six hours.

Now began a time of sharp and widespread suffering. Every-

---

[29]Bancroft, *History of Mexico,* III, 87. The subsoil of Mexico City today (1951) is slush. The splendid modern opera house has already sunk many feet below the sidewalks of the Alameda.

thing on the lower level of the buildings and houses was flooded.
Shops were closed and churches were under water. Many homes,
shops, and warehouses collapsed; costly goods were ruined, food
and provisions were destroyed. Mexico was again set upon a
lake as in the ancient days of Tenochtitlán, only that now the
waters lay along all the streets and crept up the walls of the
houses and into all the dwellings.[30] Twenty-seven thousand fled
the city while the religious orders who had novitiates in town,
the Dominicans, Franciscans, and Augustinians, removed them
to Puebla. The older houses or those of weaker (and adobe)
walls collapsed; the poorer people and those in the lower levels
of the capital were isolated and many died of hunger. Indians
came from the suburbs in their canoes carrying and selling food
and wood; bridges were built over the flooded streets from house
to house to aid communication. The thing was a major calamity,
and Archbishop and Viceroy ordered public and private prayer
and penance.

Both Archbishop and Viceroy organized in their respective
fields. The Archbishop, Francisco Manso y Zúñiga, ordered a public religious demonstration for September 24, when an ancient
image of the Blessed Virgin was carried in procession in canoes
over the waters which flooded the streets. There followed this
sacred image in boats the clergy and nobility and then the populace
of the city—what was left of it. The Archbishop ordered Mass
publicly to be said on the balconies of the houses which stood at the
crossing of streets and the people attended from below in boats,
their kneeling posture uncertain, the floor of their cathedral the
rocking bottom of their canoe. Each street corner became a
church of which the floor was water.

The high dignitaries likewise organized the necessary charities
and relief. The bishop himself took personal hand and went about
in his canoe from house to house of the more seriously stricken
carrying to the families meat, corn, beans, and bread. The Viceroy
divided the city into relief districts and organized the officials and
nobles of the city so that the most needy be sought out and that
no part of the capital be neglected. Thus necessary food was
brought to all.

---

[30]Bancroft, *op. cit.*, III, 86f.

Viceroy Cerralvo opened the public buildings to the relief of those whose houses had collapsed and these found temporary harborage here for the length of six months until finally the floods subsided. In a letter to the King, dated October 29, 1630, the Archbishop affirms that thirty thousand Indians died during the flood and that twenty thousand families became extinct; that only four hundred families remained in the capital.[31]

The Jesuits had their share both of suffering and of relief work. The professed house was severely affected but did not collapse. The Colegio Máximo, however, which was in a lower part of the city suffered more. This part of town was the first to go under water so that some of the older buildings of the college were unable to withstand the strain and collapsed. Classes had to be discontinued for many days until bridges could be built spanning the courts and connecting the different parts of the establishment. Then classes reopened and the students came in boats!

Both the professed house and the Colegio Máximo did their share in relief. The former was assigned by the Viceroy to lodge and support twelve people during the months the city was under water. Pérez de Ribas in the college took care of thirty families for four months and spent in relief and alms four thousand pesos. The loss to the college in collapsed buildings and other damage amounted to forty thousand pesos. The Jesuits suffered also in reputation. Certain enemies spread the report even through published sheets that when two years previously the six had aided in the building of the dykes and bulkheads they had been guilty of sabotage, leaving in a weakened condition certain portions of the protecting works in order to enhance the value of their own lands. Some of the unthinking accepted the calumny and for a while a certain amount of obloquy broke out against the fathers.[32]

On towards the spring of 1630 the rains stopped and the waters gradually subsided. It never rains but it pours, also in the metaphorical sense. As if Mexicans had not suffered enough, the flood was followed the next year by drought. Cattle died and pestilence

---

[31]Alegre, II, 181. Decorme, *La Obra de los Jesuitas en México en la Época Colonial, 1572-1717,* I, 350, repeats these same figures evidently taken from Alegre.

[32]*Anua* of 1629, *Archiv. Gen. Mis.,* f. 224; Alegre, II, 181.

spread apace! Later there was flood again.[33] Some were of opinion that the site of Mexico City should be changed to the higher and more salubrious levels of the valley. King Philip IV even demanded such transplantation. But the roots of the great capital had sunk too deep into the soil for so radical a transposition. Conservatism won the day, and the change was never made.[34]

All of these calamities were of course an added care and concern to our Pérez de Ribas, bearing upon his shoulders in this troubled time the responsibility of the educational center of Mexico. Consolations followed, however. Gifts helped reimburse the college for its losses and the following year a library was donated while a special wing was built to house it.[35]

Things settled down to normal once again. After the flood subsided and the drought with its pestilence had come and gone Ribas was nearing the end of his second term as rector of the Colegio Máximo. Most rectors of Jesuit colleges today look forward to the time of their relief, for the cares and the responsibilities of office are great and a man's time in such a position is seldom his own. Ribas may have felt the same. If so, he was doomed to disappointment; college president, indeed, he might cease to be; but the heavy mantle of responsibility was not his to doff at will. Able man that he was and capable of succeeding in the difficult art of ruling men, Pérez de Ribas was to be transferred from one post to another although remaining in the capital. Another community was now privileged to enjoy his kindly and prudent direction.

---

[33]Humbolt, *Political Essay on the Kingdom of New Spain*, II, 103, says the floods recurred during five years. Cf. also *anua* of 1630, *Archiv. Gen. Mis.*, t. 25, f. 227.

[34]Rivera, *Los Gobernantes de México*, I, 119; Bancroft, *op. cit.*, III, 87f.

[35]*Anua* of 1629, *loc. cit.*, f. 224.

CHAPTER XV

RIBAS BECOMES PROVINCIAL

As often happens in religious orders, once superior, always superior. When a good administrator is at hand he can be most useful. So it was with Ribas. His double term of six years at the college finished, he was sent back in 1632 to the casa profesa, but this time carrying the burden of office: he was going there to be its praepositus or rector.[1]

Ribas' duties would now be different in certain respects from those with which he was charged as rector of the Colegio. This could be in part surmised from what we have said above concerning the activities of the professed house.[2]

With regard to the Jesuit community Ribas' duties would be the same. Over the twenty-eight or thirty fathers and the dozen or so brothers of the casa he was the religious superior and as such he was responsible for the well-being of the whole house, spiritual, financial, and ministerial. Over the Jesuits of the community he had the same authority as at the Colegio though his subjects were now all formed men. Ribas may have missed his official dealing with the younger members still in training. The superior's duties here and his responsibilities personally to his community were naturally less. The professed would take care of themselves.

Financially the house was burdened with a sizeable debt whose interest had to be regularly paid. It will be remembered that the house could enjoy no set revenue, so that the daily expenses of the establishment had to be met by alms only. Pérez de Ribas would have some worries on this score, unless he was as trusting and blithesome in his supernaturalism as a Francis of Assisi or a Vincent de Paul.

Even so the house was sufficiently prosperous, especially towards the end of Ribas' regime. In 1636, for instance, the church was adorned with paintings of the saints and with tapestries and silken fabrics, and a new altar to the recently canonized Francis Xavier was dedicated. A town clock, "the finest in the

[1]*Archiv. S.J. Roman., Mex.* 4, f. 294 v.
[2]Ch. XIII.

city," was this year placed upon the tower. It was the gift of the townspeople. Alvares de Lorencana this same year built a wing onto the living quarters of the fathers at the cost of 24,000 pesos.[3] Later, an alms of twenty thousand pesos was offered on condition that Masses be said for the intention of the donor.[4]

Other energies would be expended now in the management of the church with its various and brilliant ceremonies, and in the organization and direction of ministerial activities throughout the city.

Ribas' term of office at the professed house was five years. College president from 1626 to 1632, he was superior of the casa from 1632 to 1637.

In this latter year, interestingly enough, we find Ribas back at the Colegio Máximo and again as its rector.[5] This time, however, his tenure was not more than a year or so, and the office was but a stepping stone to higher position. In 1637 he was made Provincial of New Spain by a letter of the General, Father Mutius Vitelleschi, written from Rome in October, 1637.[6] He did not take office, however, until 1638 because of a combination of circumstances equally unique and humorous.

The story of the muddle begins a few years before. In November, 1631, the forty professed seniors of the province according to age in the Society (only such were the regular constituents), met in the Colegio Máximo to convene the eleventh provincial congregation.[7] Such a meeting was prescribed in the Jesuit constitutions and was to gather every three or every six years.[8] Ribas is listed in the acts of this congregation as the thirty-first in seniority. The purposes of the meeting were to elect two procurators or representatives to go to Rome to decide on the necessity of a more general congregation and to attend in Madrid to various affairs of the province.

---

[3]*Anua* of 1636, synopsis, *Archiv. S.J. Roman., Mex.* 15, f. 471.

[4]*Colección de Cartas Inéditas,* Vitelleschi to Ayerve, Oct. 30, 1637.

[5]*Ibid.*

[6]*Ibid.* If there is any obscurity in this letter concerning the status of Ribas in 1637 it seems to be removed by the acts of the Provincial Congregation of that year which refer to him as rector of the Colegio Máximo.

[7]Alegre, II, 189.

[8]*Constitutiones Societatis Jesu, pars* VIII, *cap.* II and III.

The fathers who were elected to travel to Europe were Tomás Domínguez and Floriano de Ayerve, erstwhile provincial of New Granada and former missionary on the west coast. Among the petitions to be asked of the General was this: that the term of the provincials be restricted to three years which was according to the constitutions of the Society and had been customary prior to 1602 when a dispensation was made for Mexico because of the great distance from Rome.[9]

The procurators went off then to Rome with their petitions, and the one concerning the limitation of the provincialate was granted by the General, who appointed, as a matter of fact, Ayerve himself as the new incumbent beginning with the year 1632.

Ayerve returned with letters to this effect and with letters likewise for Luis de Bonifaz, former missionary of Sinaloa, who just preceded Ribas as rector of the professed house. These letters for Bonifaz were to be delivered after three years, namely in 1635, and were in effect the official appointment of Bonifaz as provincial to succeed Ayerve. Now, when the three years had elapsed Ayerve failed to deliver these letters to Bonifaz so that no new provincial was forthcoming, nor yet the following year of 1636.

The fathers of the province may have been disappointed that their request of a three-year term, seemingly granted three years before, was not in practice being carried out. The General in Rome was moreover both disappointed and mystified when he learned that Ayerve and not Bonifaz was after 1635 still acting as provincial. Ayerve now broke down and admitted what he had done; he confessed to withholding the official letters appointing Bonifaz his successor. He offered as excuse that the old missionary, Luis de Bonifaz, was in poor health and unable to govern![10]

The letter of appointment being now known in Mexico, Bonifaz took up his duties in 1637, while in Rome this fact was unknown so that the General wrote appointing Pérez de Ribas as pro-

---

[9]Alegre, loc. cit.

[10]Alegre, II, 205ff. offers another version of Ayerve's motives, but judging from Vitelleschi's letters to Ayerve his view seems incorrect. Cf. Colección de Cartas Inéditas, letter of Oct. 30, 1637.

vincial. "It seemed, then, that there were three provincials, Bonifaz who was so acting, Ayerve who was getting the letters, and Ribas whose appointment was unknown in Mexico." Ribas was modest enough amidst the confusion. He was not at all anxious to assume office, wishing the honor (and also the burden) to be carried for two more years by Father Bonifaz, his old friend and fellow missioner. "In the predicament occasioned by two friends charitably bowing each other in and out of office," a provincial consultation was called with its resultant verdict that Ribas was to hold office from 1638 to 1641 while Luis de Bonifaz was to succeed him.[11]

So it was done and so did our quondam college president and recent superior of the professed house take up the office of provincial, the highest that could be given amongst the Jesuits of New Spain.[12]

The organization which Ribas now headed had about reached the pinnacle of its prestige and prosperity. The number of Jesuits in Mexico had, as we have seen, been continually on the increase up to 1628 when they numbered 382.[13] Almost a decade later there were 378 exclusive of novices. This figure includes 184 priests, the largest number after a steady rise since the province began in 1572.[14] The year Ribas became provincial there was an increase of six: sixteen had been admitted, while ten had died.[15] Ribas ruled as provincial over all the Jesuit missions and communities of New Spain. The latter numbered twenty-three.[16]

To him, as head of the whole province, these men were completely submitted, in a submission which surpassed in quality and in quantity that usually given. If his subjects lived up to the spirit of their rule of life they must obey this provincial of theirs "not only . . . in performing exteriorly the things which he enjoins . . . but also they must endeavor to be resigned in-

---

[11]Alegre, II, 207.

[12]Father Jerome V. Jacobsen in "The Chronicle of Pérez de Ribas," *Mid-America*, XX (Apr., 1938), 81-95, gives a humorously colorful account of the impasse, from which the above is partly taken.

[13]See *supra*, pp. 80-81.

[14]*Anua* of 1636, synopsis, *Archiv. S.J. Roman., Mex.* 15, f. 470.

[15]*Anua* of 1638, *loc. cit.*, f. 476.

[16]*Anua* of 1628, *loc. cit.*, f. 141.

teriorly and to have a true abnegation of their own will and judgment, conforming their will and judgment wholly to what the superior wills and judges, in all things where there appears no sin . . . " and "denying with a certain kind of blind obedience any contrary opinion or judgment of their own."[17] This sort of submission argued practically complete power of Ribas over his men and it surpassed any other kind of obedience ever given before, because the Jesuit founder was the great propagator in the modern Church of obedience of the judgment, of the much malinged virtue of blind obedience, which indeed is so seldom blind.

It would be unscientific and unpsychological, and therefore unhistorical, to presume that all Ribas' subjects lived up to the perfection of their rule. Human nature remains human, and it seldom is able to hold consistently to the perfection of a high ideal. But even allowing for certain imperfections on the part of many or most of the subjects of Ribas, one might with fair probability venture the reflection that Spaniards or mestizos of the early seventeenth century would render their superior a larger share of interior obedience than would certain northern types of the middle twentieth century.

However, granting that numbers of Ribas' subjects missed the high and gilded pinnacle of the ideal, they still would yield him an exterior and even a willing respect. The power he exercised, therefore, was great, as is that of every Jesuit provincial, but it was gently wielded, unobstrusive, and happily acceded to on the part of the subjects in general. This alleged submission of Ribas' subjects was according to the rule and constitution that they had freely submitted to. The normal Jesuit subject is content thus "to yield up his own powers to bind and dedicate himself to God."

When we look into the prestige enjoyed by the whole Jesuit group at this time in New Spain and examine the personal quality of ever so many of the individuals we can better appreciate the position which Ribas occupied, albeit quietly, humbly Christian, deliberate, and with no consciousness of personal importance or

---

[17]Ignatius Loyola, *Summary of the Constitutions,* 31 and 35.

of power enjoyed and wielded. In this year of 1638 there were seventeen colleges and six residences, including the novitiate, but not counting the missions of the north. These latter were expanding and spreading constantly and the fame of their success resounded not only throughout New Spain and the Americas, but it leaped across the ocean and penetrated into the courts and capitals of Europe.

In Mexico City Jesuit fortunes had been rising and Ribas stepped into office shortly after both of the important Jesuit houses in the city had been materially augmented. We have spoken of the improvements to the professed house and the church in 1636 while Ribas was superior there. In the same year a dormitory was constructed for the Colegio Máximo, which contained rooms not for the students, however, but for their Jesuit professors. The cost of this was 8,000 in gold, while 4,550 was spent in the interior adornment of the college church. This same year, which seems to have been a golden twelvemonth, a new piece of property in the country, a farm yielding corn and grain, was willed to the Order. It bore an income of a thousand a year.[18] All this flow of good fortune was two years before Ribas' incumbency and while he was superior of the casa. We should say that his provincialate fell upon growing and prosperous times.

Since Pérez de Ribas had been so important a factor in the organization and spread of the missions of the north it would have been expected that as provincial he would exercise a very especial interest in the continued spread and success of these history-making institutions. As a matter of fact, his correspondence shows that the affairs of the missions entered importantly into his concerns. Ribas had it in mind to write the history of these missions and it is very probable that he had long ago begun his famous *Historia de los Triumphos*. If not this, he may already have finished certain chapters of his manuscript on the history of Sinaloa which was never completed and never published. He would be then as provincial particularly interested in the north.

Since Ribas had left the missions late in 1619 they had ad-

---

[18]*Anua* of 1636, synopsis, *loc. cit.,* f. 470. The *anua* lists the articles which were acquired by the college church: ten sets of vestments, silver candelabra, gold-inlaid cruets, eight silver cups, a silver cross, etc.

vanced apace. On the west coast they had marched far up Río Yaqui, passed over a divide into the Sonora Valley to the northwest and the valley of the Río Bavispe to the northeast. New tens of thousands had been added to the number of the baptized. In the mountains and up along the plains to the east progress continued: the southern Tarahumares, after many setbacks and delays, were being gradually penetrated. Ribas had watched this development with the keenest interest, and now from 1638 as provincial his was to be the directing authority of all of it. Provincials hardly ever visited the missions personally because of the great distance. This work was done by official vicars called Visitors. Rodrigo de Cabredo, however, did visit Durango in December, 1610,[19] and Juan Laurencio did the same in 1622. In this latter year Ribas, the provincial's secretary, may have accompanied him.[20]

In the fall of 1638, letters of a nature both to console and worry came down from the Tepehuán country, from Santiago-Papasquiaro, written by Father Gaspar de Contreras, who had just been appointed by Ribas superior of the Tepehuán mission. The Tarahumares are ripe for the gospel, the father urged, and missionaries ought to be sent to them as soon as possible. The land is fertile and they are asking for missionaries, says Contreras in his missive of August 5. These their just desires ought to be satisfied. The Tarahumares are serving the Spaniards in the mines at Parral and the Spaniards barter with Indians exchanging cotton, garments, and other wares for corn. These Tarahumares have been greatly tamed since the olden days so that, unarmed and unescorted, the Spaniards can go among them. And also many now are dying from the plague without baptism or without the sacraments. "This flock is ours," presses Contreras, "and we are responsible for their baptism."[21]

This Contreras urged in the fall of 1638 and Pérez de Ribas was the last man in the world to turn a deaf ear to such representations. Ribas acted the following year by sending three missionaries to the Tarahumares. Indeed, the Provincial in listen-

---

[19]*Anua* of 1610, *Archiv. S.J. Roman., Mex.* 14, f. 576.

[20]Alegre, II, 166.

[21]*Archiv*. *Gen. Mis.,* t. 25, 282 and 284f.

ing to these appeals of Contreras opened the lower Tarahumar
country as a permanent organized unit of the mission system.
The Tepehuán revolt of 1616 had put off indefinitely the plans
for permanent padres among the Tarahumares, but now in 1639
Ribas was able to put the mission on a solid basis by sending
Fathers José Pascual and Gerónimo de Figueroa up into the coun-
try. Soon Cornelio Beudin arrived and labored for ten years here.
He was killed in the uprising of 1650.[22] In 1641 Ribas named
Figueroa as superior of the unit and it was officially called Baja
Tarahumara.[23] Ribas from the capital had founded a new mis-
sion unit.

As for the Tepehuanes, Contreras writes, hardly ever does one
encounter a member of this nation but he wears his rosary beads
around his neck. This latter piece of information was encouraging
to the Provincial, because the previous year Contreras reported
that in Zape, seventy miles north, the cacique Don Pedro, brother
of the rebellious Don Felipe, urged by a hechicero, was stirring up
trouble and preaching revolt. Ribas took a direct hand in this. He
sent a letter to Contreras to be delivered in his name to the Indians at Zape and instructed Contreras to give word of the danger
to Captain Barrasa. Don Pedro was placated, apologized, and
did penance. The trouble was past and both Contreras at the
mission and Ribas in Mexico City breathed more easily.[24]

It did not detract from Ribas' satisfaction that the missions
were progressing well along the west coast. Lorenzo de Figueroa
wrote in June, 1639, that all was going nicely among those missions and he gave figures for the Huite nation, among whom
close to nine hundred had been baptized that year while 374 had
been married in the Church. In Sonora, says this same letter,
Fathers Castaño and Pantoja were baptizing in large numbers.[25]

---

[22]*Noticias de las misiones sacadas de la anua del Padre José Pascual,
Año de 1651, Doc. Hist. Mex.*, series 4, vol. 3, pp. 179f. Beudin is called
Godínez in this document.

[23]Bannon, "The Jesuits in Sonora, 1620-1687," MS., ch. VIII. Cf. also
Christelow, "Father Joseph Neumann, Jesuit Missionary to the Tarahumares," *The Hispanic American Historical Review*, XIX (Nov. 1939),
p. 427. Also, Dunne, *Early Jesuit Missions in Tarahumara*, ch. VI.

[24]*Archiv. Gen. Mis.*, t. 25, f. 282.

[25]*Loc. cit.*, f. 288.

During the sixteen-thirties there had been a slowing down of the rapid and splendid advance on the west coast which in the twenties had traveled up along the Yaqui River and gone into the Nébomes, Pima Baja, and into the Opatas. As socius to Laurencio during the earlier twenties Ribas would have some influence here and as a matter of fact during this time the missions went on apace. As rector of the Colegio and superior of the casa Ribas would be farther removed from central influence regarding mission policy. It was exactly during these thirties that there was a slowing down. The missions could not advance without missionaries, and so great was the need in the south (so the provincials thought) that men could not be sent to the northern establishments, and they were not.[26]

When Pérez de Ribas became provincial his interest and action were immediately shown on the west coast as over the divide. He wrote a letter to the General in favor of the missions. We do not possess the letter, but we have a copy of the answer from which the spirit of Ribas' missive is evident. Father General Vitelleschi replied October 30, 1639, in part as follows: "I have that appreciation of the missions of the province, and especially of those of Sinaloa, which they deserve. And not once alone, but often have I spoken of them in a spirit of especial esteem. I know well the need they have of many ministers of the gospel and so far as I am concerned I shall lend aid in procuring them. I ask Your Reverence that on your part you come to the assistance of the missions with all care and diligence, sending from the other parts of the province laborers who, as I am informed, are superfluous in some colleges, but are deficient in the missions. Likewise I beg of you that you supply to those who labor in so holy a work what is necessary for them with all charity and generosity. Likewise I enjoin all to promote so glorious an enterprise and exhort the study of the Indian languages."[27]

Mutius Vitelleschi certainly responded with equal or even surpassing enthusiasm to Ribas' plea for the Sinaloa missions and the latter could feel himself not only encouraged, but justified in whatever vigorous methods he might wish to em-

---

[26]Cf. Bannon, op. cit., ch. VI.
[27]Colección de Cartas Inéditas, Vitelleschi to Ribas, Oct. 30, 1639.

ploy for their help. Ribas even wanted to name a vice-provincial who might visit the missions of the north and enjoy provincialate powers for their government. The General, however, considered this too great a departure from the close-fitting organization of the Society and wrote to Ribas to that effect.[28] But since the ground to be covered by the provincial in his official visitations was so great the General speaks of a possible division of the province and asks Ribas to bring it before his consultors. Nothing came of this suggestion, however, and the province of New Spain was never divided.

But the missions did go ahead, especially in Sonora. The very first year of Ribas' provincialate Father Bartolomé de Castaño rode into the northern Sonora country following Lorenzo de Cárdenas, who had made the first entrada some years previous. Then in 1639 Pedro Pantoja came to aid Castaño and the latter was able, together with Pantoja, to begin the baptisms of the Pimas and Ópatas up the Sonora River with their pueblos of Ures, Babiacora, Guepaca, and the rest. The following year this far-northern section was formed by Ribas into a separate administrative unit, called the *Rectorado de San Francisco Javier,* comprising the *partidos* or sections of Comoripa, Aibino, Batuco, Ures, and Sonora. Seven missionaries administered to these groups of the Ópata and Pima Baja Indians under the superiorship of Pantoja himself. In 1641 in the neighboring unit, called the *Rectorado de San Ignacio,* the infant baptisms amounted to thirteen thousand, which was equal to the very finest years of the sixteen-twenties.[29]

Not for nothing had Ribas been an old missioner; as provincial he did as much for the missions as he had been able to accomplish actually in the field.

Another instance which brought Ribas as provincial into the

---

[28]*Ibid.*
[29]Alegre, II, 222; Bannon, *op. cit.,* ch. VII. The *rectorado* was the chief unit of this mission organization whose superior was called the rector. In each *rectorado* were *partidos* or sections administered by a missionary. Each *partido* had pueblos and villages called *visitas.* In these latter the padre did not reside, but visited regularly (hence the name) to say Mass and administer the sacraments.

direct and intimate concern of the missions was the royal cédula or decree of December 23, 1637, from the King to the Viceroy. The Viceroy was instructed to look into the matter of a possible division of the northern bishopric, that of Durango, and to send a detailed account of the condition of the country. Viceroy Lópe Díaz de Armendáriz, Marqués de Cadereyta, reissued the instructions on August 5, 1638, and sent copies to the Bishop, the Dean, and to the Chapter of Durango, to the Commissary-general of the Franciscans, and to the Provincial of the Jesuits. Eight questions were to be answered including the size of the herds developed in the missions, the fertility of the land, the population of Indians, and taxes to the king.[30]

Ribas gathered around him at the Colegio Máximo a group of former missionaries like himself and they drew up an accurate answer to the eight points of query. Ten former missionaries sat around the council table and the list as preserved in the official document is headed by the veteran Pedro Méndez and closed by Juan de Ardeñas. They had both worked in Sinaloa. Others there like Andrés López and Martín de Egurro had worked in the mountains or on the plains east of the divide. The reply is dated September 12, 1638, and covers over nine closely printed folio pages. It is an excellent source of information on the state of the missions at that time.[31]

While Father Pedro de Velasco, likewise former missionary, was in Rome in 1640 acting as representative to the General from the province of New Spain, he handed in among others the petition that Mexican Jesuits be allowed to open a new mission in (Lower) California. Vitelleschi replied by a letter of April 6, 1640, in which he approved the proposal and praised the fine spirit of the fathers, especially that of Father de Velasco, who had offered to go himself, but prudently deferred decision until the matter should be more thoroughly discussed.[32] And the General otherwise, independently of Ribas, shows himself in this corres-

---

[30]Bandelier-Hackett, *Historical Documents Relating to New Mexico, Nueva Vizcaya and Approaches Thereto to 1773*, III, 94f.

[31]Cf. Bandelier-Hackett, *op. cit.*, III, 95ff. For a full account see Bannon, *op. cit.*, ch. VII.

[32]*Colección de Cartas Inéditas*, letter of April 6, 1640.

pondence exceedingly interested in the missions. We would expect as much, for under Vitelleschi the Jesuits were carrying on a most notable missionary activity all over the world. Indeed, missionary labors were considered among the most important duties of the Society, then as now.

Other things nearer home pertaining to government likewise occupied Ribas' attention as provincial and stimulated his interest. In Vera Cruz there was a residence and now a donation came in, a considerable estate, for the founding of a college. This was early in 1639, and must have delighted Ribas, but little did he then realize what sharp arrows and heavy slings of outrageous fortune were to come upon the province of New Spain, occasioned but not caused by this rich donation.

By letter of January 30, 1639, the donor himself, Don Fernando de la Serna Váldez, wrote to Ribas to inform him as to the revenues of the estate he was bequeathing for a college in Vera Cruz. It was a sheep run and had now for many years supported 30,000 head yielding an annual revenue of 10,000 pesos.[33] This was a grand gift, and a college at Vera Cruz could well carry on with this support; but within four years such a storm was raised against the Jesuits over this donation that it would have been well had the gift never been made. It was the Bishop of Puebla, in whose diocese the estate existed, Don Juan de Palafox y Mendoza, who blew up a very hurricane of trouble and persecution which was to resound over the whole of Mexico, fly across the seas, and rage in fury even over Europe. The Bishop was abetted by Jesuit imprudence. But more of this anon.

Ribas indeed had a busy life. The care of many affairs and responsibilities flowed daily in upon him. Much of his time too must needs be taken up with travel. Each year all of the twenty-three houses must be visited and each of his three hundred and eighty subjects spoken with and listened to. Troubles of finance, troubles of administration, troubles of conscience were poured into his paternal ear. Consolations too were his; not of finance, it is true, but of administration and especially of matters spiritual. For according to the Jesuit rule the subject must manifest his

---

[33]*Anua* of 1639, *Archiv. Gen. Mis.*, t. 25, f. 479; Alegre, II, 223.

conscience to his superior and while such manifestation was given regularly to the superior of the house, it could be and often was made to the provincial.

The consolations of this provincial, Pérez de Ribas, can be more properly appreciated when we realize the large number of extraordinary men over whom he ruled. It was during his provincialate that Father Ildefonso Guerrero died at the Colegio Máximo. He was the nephew of the founder of this Jesuit center and son of the wealthy Agustín Guerrero who had given the lad 4,000 pesos a year spending money. All of this the boy left behind in order to join the Jesuit ranks bound to a vow of poverty. There was the high-born Pedro de Velasco, son of the Viceroy, Pedro de Velasco II. As a young priest, the Jesuit Velasco went up to the missions of the west coast and did good work on the upper Sinaloa among the Chicoratos and Cahuemetos. Recalled to the capital he was engaged in preaching and in teaching. Finally he too was made provincial only a few years after Ribas' term of office.

There was the famous Luis de Molina, gifted with an extraordinary eloquence and the most famous preacher in the capital. Alegre says that his virtue reached as high as his voice. Then, Pérez de Ribas had for subject one who was undoubtedly among the greatest of the missionaries who labored and endured in the Americas, Father Pedro Méndez. Méndez had spent with slight interruptions almost half a century in the missions, and traveled two thousand miles on mule-back, passed through tribes who spoke forty different dialects of which Méndez preached in five. Pedro Méndez, sunk beneath the weight of over fourscore summers, died just five years after Ribas left office.[34]

There was Vincente de Aguila, missionary in Sinaloa; there were Cornelio Beudin and Jacopo Basilio, martyrs of the Tarahumares; there was Ribas' own predecessor in office, Luis de Bonifaz; there was the mystic and author, Miguel Godínez; there was the eminent man of letters, Andrés de Valencia. Add to these Pedro Navarro, Juan Esteban, Baltazar López, and

---

[34]*Archiv. Gral. MS. sin fecha.* For a fine interpretation of the career of Méndez see Bannon, "Black-Robe Frontiersman: Pedro Méndez, S.J.", *Hispanic American Historical Review,* XXVIII (February, 1947), 61-86.

Gabriel Espinoza. These last three died between 1643 and 1651 of the plague, caught in nursing the sick and dying.[35] And so the list could be indefinitely prolonged.[36] Nothing there was that Ribas could not know of these extraordinary men. Their heart and their soul, their trials and their aspirations, could equally be laid bare before him. Such inner richness consoled the Provincial for the trials and responsibilities of office.

Ribas was provincial when in 1640 there took place the splendid entrance into Mexico City of the seventeenth viceroy, Cabrera y Bobadilla, Duke of Escalona. "The young duke was a direct descendant of the great Braganza of Portugal, King Manuel of the Golden Age. He was the first grandee of Spain to become viceroy and a Knight of the Golden Fleece. He was a young and gallant courtier, proud, elegant, blasé, with white forehead, rosy cheeks, and soft silky beard."

The Duke embarked from Cádiz in the glitter and profusion of effete royalty. A hundred pack-horses and a hundred saddle-mules carried his baggage to the wharves while it required eight coaches to carry himself and his suite—family, chaplains, and servants. His ship was laden with all things that were good: "two thousand hens, a dozen calves, and two hundred lambs; there were also six huge chests of sweetmeats, innumerable kegs of fruit pastes, and an enormous quantity of biscuit, hams, rice, macaroni, lentils, chestnuts, chick-peas, wines, and raisins." Arrived in New Spain at the fort of San Juan de Ulúa and port of Vera Cruz he was escorted into the city "midst the roar of a royal salute . . . in a felluca canopied with carmine damask, clad in suit of white silk embroidered with silver. Two trumpeters in green satin livery, with carmine damask pennants on their clarinets, accompanied him, along with a troop of dependents and militia."

Embarked from Spain early in April the Duke and his party were completing the final unit of their journey early in August. Along the time-honored route of centuries the viceregal cavalcade journeyed from Vera Cruz to Mexico City. Up from the miasmic and feverish lowlands of the coast they mounted thou-

---

[35]Decorme, *La Obra de los Jesuitas*, I, 336.
[36]Alegre, II, *libro* VII, *passim*.

sands of feet through Soledad de Doblado, Paso del Macho, and
Córdoba to the salubrious elevations of Orizaba, whence that
graceful cone of an extinct volcano, towering and ever white,
spoke to the Duke of the physical enchantments of North America.
Soon the cavalcade would pass between the glittering cone of
Popocatepetl and the serene Iztaccihuatl, to descend into the ancient valley of the Aztecs. The outgoing viceroy, Lópe Díaz de
Armendáriz, Marqués de Cadereyta, on his way to the coast, met
the incoming Duke at Otumba. It was the etiquette and ancient
custom of the age that this wayside meeting take place. "With
ceremonious punctilio both viceroys descended from their coaches
at the same instant. Escalona received Cadereyta in his own
carriage and side by side they rode back into Otumba."

The capital had voted 40,000 pesos for the reception of the
Duke, and the entry was set for August 28. As he drew near the
city thousands strewed the way to acclaim him and to shout out
their desire for a generous government. As the brilliant company
arrived at a floral arch the town council bade the Viceroy welcome
and presented him with two steeds, the best in the land. Mean-
while there came forth to escort him a cavalcade of musicians,
bailiffs, and knights; the professors and students of the royal
University of Mexico, and the various and sundry officials of
the city. At the church of Santo Domingo before the gates of the
city the procession passed through an arch of ninety feet erected
for the occasion, its facade crowded with figures of the gods of
antiquity and with symbolic representations of the major virtues.
Here after the new viceroy had taken his oath to guard the civic
privileges and protect the Kingdom of New Spain, the gates were
flung open and the Duke entered his domain.

Roofs, balconies, and thoroughfares were solid with humanity
except for a hardly maintained passage for the cavalcade to approach the cathedral. Here another arch had been erected, the
clergy chanted the *Te Deum,* and within the basilica oratory,
poetry, felicitations, and prayers followed in a rich succession
until sundown. At dusk a million candles sparkled their welcome
to the Duke.

This was only a beginning. The celebrations went on for two

whole months and only then did the new viceroy turn himself to the cares of state and the administration of the kingdom.[37]

Though we do not read of it, Pérez de Ribas as the Jesuit Provincial, would be among the notables to welcome the Viceroy, while the fathers of the professed house and the students of the Colegio Máximo would take a humble part in the magnificent affair.

But, a high-placed churchman had come over with the Duke of Escalona. He had been designated by the King as Bishop of Puebla and as he was a man of notable parts and stood high in the royal favor, he was soon to mount higher, even to the humiliation and downfall of the new viceroy; he was to stand on the gilded pinnacle of the glory of the New World. His name was Juan de Palafox y Mendoza, Bishop of Puebla.

In the meantime Pérez de Ribas finished his years as provincial in 1641 to be succeeded in office by his old confrère of the west coast missions, Luis de Bonifaz. Ribas could not, however, shake off the cloak of authority He was returned to the Colegio Máximo to begin there his third period as rector.[38]

---

[37]Priestley, *The Coming of the White Man*, pp. 162ff. The above account is condensed from these pages of most interesting detail, taken originally from Génaro García, *Don Juan de Palafox y Mendoza, obispo de Puebla y Osma, visitador y virrey de Nueva España*, ch. IV. For the Viceroy's later troubles with the doughty Palafox, Bishop of Puebla, cf. Rivera, *Los Gobernantes de México*, I, 176ff.

[38]Alegre, II, 239.

CHAPTER XVI

RIBAS WRITES A BOOK

In a large university of the West there used to be a professor of history who perhaps broke all world records in size of classes and in number of those tutored. This statement is supported by the fact that over a period of many scholastic years the numbers attending ranged from 800 odd in a semester to the record figure of 1,285![1] In the autumn of every year this benign personality used to carry down to class from the top floor of the library a great book bound in sheepskin containing between its covers 756 double-columned pages. The pupils who sat on the front row of the great hall could read upon the back of its cover: *Historia de las missiones de Nueva España, Madrid, 1645.*

The professor held high this book before his curious pupils, shook it at them, and said something like this: "Here is one of the greatest books ever written in the West." It is the work of our Andrés Pérez de Ribas, and its full title reads: *Historia de los Triumphos de Nuestra Santa Fee Entre Gentes los Mas Barbaros y Fieros del Nuevo Orbe,* or *History of the Triumphs of Our Holy Faith Among Nations the Most Wild and Barbarous of the New World.* It was published in Madrid in 1645 and achieved in its day a great success, but the known copies of the old edition are now very rare.[2]

This book, the *Los Triumphos,* was being written while Pérez de Ribas was engaged in all the work of administration we have spoken of in the foregoing chapters.

Like the Roman poet Horace, he carved in hard metal and in bronze. Many a monument of actual stone or iron has either been toppled over or stands in obscurity and neglect. Many a book has and will be written either to live for a day, or to be merely listed

---

[1]We are referring to the course entitled "History of the Americas" given over a long period at the University of California by Dr. Herbert Eugene Bolton.

[2]Recently there has been made a reprint of the ancient classic published by Editorial Layac, Mexico, 1944. The 1645 edition may be found in North America in the Bancroft Library, University of California; in the Library of Congress; in the Newberry Library, Chicago; and in the Father Cuevas Collection in Mexico City.

in learned bibliographies. It is not so with Ribas' *Los Triumphos*. Appearing at first in 1645 as a history of important missions in the New World, after three hundred years the book lives to the profit of mankind. It could be easily read for pleasure and entertainment as a fascinating story which happens to be true, for it is history. Actually, wherever it rests in libraries it is consulted by scholars of various types—historians, ethnologists, geographers—that they might draw from it ancient lore and the abundant knowledge of the past which it contains.

If not in a preface, the author has clearly indicated in the course of his work the reasons for his writing. From the eleventh chapter of his third book we quote his words: "This history is written principally for our fathers of the Society of Jesus that they be encouraged to employ themselves in these holy missions and in order that they learn the marvels which God is able to perform in conquering all difficulties which occur in the winning over of nations as proud and as rebellious as these."[3] Ribas has in mind here his own great successes on the Fuerte River and the conversion of the rebellious Suaqui nation in 1605. When he wrote these words he may have just finished the story of his enthusiastic welcome at their hands on his coming to their pueblos.

In the first chapters of the seventh book Ribas returns at length to the theme of the excellence of the work on these missions. He devotes the whole first chapter of this seventh book to demonstrating that these missionary labors are as fine and as important as any in Europe and in the second chapter he shows how fit subjects these Indians are for receiving the Faith. In the third he gives an answer to various difficulties or objections to the work of the missions which might be brought forward. The miraculous phenomena which allegedly occur he offers as an incentive to the future missionary and he points out the vastness of the field to be cultivated. In this connection, interestingly enough, he tells how this mission field stands at the very gateway to California.

The then unknown and mysterious lands of California already intrigued the old-time missionary Pérez de Ribas, for in chapter twelve of this seventh book he prints a letter of the Viceroy to the

---

[3]III, 11.

Jesuit Provincial concerning the advisability of missions on the Peninsula. He tells how in 1642 Father Jacinto Cortés at the instance of Captain Luis Centín de Cañas crossed over from the mainland to Lower California and made a report on the conditions there. California had gripped the imagination of soldier and missionary alike.

Again in chapter eleven Ribas is clear as to his purpose in the composition of his great work. He says here that the purpose of his *Los Triumphos* "is that it become known how in the glorious work of the preaching of the Gospel to these tribes, no matter how wild and fierce they may be, the end aimed at is being accomplished. For it is manifest that the spiritual fruits of these conquests are not less happy nor less abundant than those gathered in among other nations of the greatest name, nations the most noble and renowned of all the world."

Finally in the epilogue which is the fifteenth chapter of the twelfth book the historian returns to his theme and reminds the reader that the grand work is still going on as he writes. He swings back to the glories of martyrdom, mentioning the eight Jesuits who were killed in what is now the state of Virginia, the eight who fell among the Tepehuanes, and the three who were murdered by savages in Sinaloa. He speaks again of "the vast lands of California," a virgin field for the desires of the most ambitious missionary. In a last chapter, unartistically tacked on to the epilogue (like Gibbon he seems to have found it hard to give it up) he reverts to the same theme. May these chapters foster missionaries, he concludes, in order that "such fine labors and such glorious victories continue indefinitely." No one in that century, the seventeenth, wrote for the mere imparting of knowledge, except perhaps Descartes. Such singleness of purpose is a product rather of the twentieth century and is rare even in that "enlightened" age.

Is this a work, therefore, primarily of propaganda and consequently to be distrusted? The man has ulterior motives, a critic might aver, an "ax to grind." Or is it a work of spiritual edification, from whose fertile if scientifically unwholesome soil legend has luxuriously sprouted throughout all the centuries of Christianity's existence? A careful examination of its pages shows that this is not the case with *The Triumphs of the Faith*. Ribas throughout his writing was actuated by a strong desire to tell the truth. But as a matter of fact, what defects there are in the book come partly from this intention to stimulate and edify. That the defects are so few and the qualities on the other hand so great shows Ribas, for his age and environment, an extraordinary man.

Before examining the book critically and more at length it might be well first to describe the work, for its scope is vast. The *Los Triumphos,* or *The Triumphs of the Faith* as we can call it, covers minutely the first half-century, from 1591 to 1643, of one of the largest and most successful, if not one of the most important, missionary developments in the history of Christianity since the Reformation. During sixteen years, as we have seen, Pérez de Ribas was one of the pivotal units of this development; during the rest of the time he was close to it, morally if not geographically. Our author carries the story of the missions of the West from Río Sinaloa, where they began with Tapia and Martín Pérez, up along the coast; he carries them over the rivers which drop into the Gulf of California, up hundreds of miles into the Sonora Valley. This the most important part of his story he covers in the first seven books each divided into many chapters.

With the eighth book begins the *secunda parte,* or second part, comprising five books. Here is narrated the development of the mission system as it worked in through the mountains, north and south, the rugged Sierra Madre of the West, and as it spread out over the eastern plains in present Durango and Coahuila. It is this portion which includes the story of the great Tepehuán revolt which gave eight Jesuit martyrs to the Church with a Dominican and a Franciscan. Ribas desired to round out twelve books according to the mystic number, but his story was really finished with the eleventh. He breaks the unity and also the continuity of his work by this added twelfth book in which he treats of the Florida mission in the fifteen-sixties and its martyrs, of the transient missions about San Luis de la Paz, finally winding up with the epilogue and *fin de opus.*

The historian had therefore a grand story to tell and grandly did he tell it. So far as its importance is concerned, both as to mission history and the development of a colonial frontier, there is little to equal it in the New World, if we exclude the vast numbers baptized shortly after the conquest by the Franciscans when a sort of tribal movement into the Church took place.[4] In South America we have the famous Jesuit Reductions of Paraguay and the missions of the north country of present Argentina. The former became justly renowned for the unique success of their organization. Here was a sort of socialized state in complete isolation from Europeans, which enjoyed an almost idyllic career. The Paraguay missions have achieved an enviable record in history. In numbers of converts they seem to have surpassed the developments Ribas had to record. One survey of Paraguay, understating, says that "in two decades thirteen mission stations had been established and the converts were estimated at about forty thousand."[5] In the neighborhood of Tucumán, in present Argentina, Father Alonzo de Bargana alone baptized in the single year of 1585 two thousand four hundred and twenty-four. The next year he did the same for more than four thousand, to which were added almost three thousand the following six months.[6] According to the anua of 1610 for Paraguay and Argentina, Tucumán had eighty thousand Christian Indians in that year,[7] while the anua for 1611 gives the fine number of 110,000 Christian Indians for these missions.[8]

But there was no contemporary Jesuit historian to write and publish the story. There seems to have been nobody like our Pérez de Ribas to organize the detailed narration of this splendid work into a brilliant history. If the French Black Robes in Canada

---

[4]Cf. Ricard, La 'Conquête Spirituelle' du Mexique, p. 112. The pioneer Franciscan historian Motolinía estimated that 5,000,000 were baptized between 1524 and 1536. Ibid.

[5]Jones, An Introduction to Hispanic American History, p. 169. Rippy and Nelson in Crusaders of the Jungle give no exact figures, but remark that in 1742 the Jesuits could place an Indian army of 40,000 archers in the field (p. 240). The Jesuit Charlevoix in The History of Paraguay gives no figures.

[6]Astrain, Historia de la Compañía de Jesús en la Asistencia de España, IV, 609 f. Astrain gives 114,599 as the number of neophytes in the Paraguay reductions in 1702. Op. cit., VI, 670.

[7]Documentos para Historia Argentina, XIX, 41.

[8]Ibid., p. 84.

were fortunate to have their Parkman, and Junipero Serra his Palóu, so were the early Jesuit missions on the west coast of North America fortunate to have their Andrés Pérez de Ribas.

It is true, we have the instructive and adventurous story of the German Jesuit missionary of South America, Martin Dobrizhoffer. His *An Account of the Abipones and Equestrian People of Paraguay* was translated from the Latin in three volumes in 1822.[9] But this tells of a wild and savage people rather than of a mission organization. Charlevoix's *History of Paraguay* is not specifically on the missions nor is it greatly detailed concerning them. The record of heroic labors with suffering and martyrdom of the North American French Jesuits in Canada is well known. The above mentioned French Jesuit Charlevoix[10] and after him the American Protestant Francis Parkman,[11] have made the Canadian missionary story famous; but it is also known that the number of the converts in Canada was relatively small, even if the extent of territory ultimately covered was large.

The Franciscan historian José Arlegui wrote of the sixteenth-and seventeenth-century Franciscan missions in northern Mexico[12] and Luis Gerónimo de Oré, O. F. M., narrates the history of the early Franciscan martyrs in Florida,[13] while Father Maynard Geiger, O. F. M., has recently given an account of the Franciscan missions in Florida after the Jesuits had failed.[14] In the seventeenth century in New Mexico the Franciscans baptized their tens of

---

[9]London: John Murray, Albemarle Street, 1822. There are accounts of a limited field in manuscript, such as Father Antonio de Montoya's *Conquista Espiritual.* Cf. Astrain, *op. cit.,* V, 574, notes 1 and 2.

[10]*History and General Description of New France.*

[11]*Jesuits in North America in the Seventeenth Century.*

[12]*Crónica de la Provincia de S. P. N. S. Francisco de Zacatecas.*

[13]*Relacion de los Mártires que ha habido en las Provincias de la Florida.* This work was published in Madrid in 1931 by Fray Atanasio López, O.F.M., under the title: *Relación Histórica de la Florida Escrito en el Siglo XVII.* Cf. Geiger, "The Martyrs of Florida, 1513-1616," who under the latter title translated and published Oré's work in *Franciscan Studies,* no. 18, July, 1936.

[14]*The Franciscan Conquest of Florida, 1573-1618.* One report of 1595, twenty-two years after the founding of the missions, places the number of baptized of five missions as something over 1,500, *ibid.,* p. 65.

thousands.[15] But for sheer onward marching success both in territory and in numbers the story which Ribas tells in most of the books of his *Los Triumphos* seems to carry the day with regard to early mission historiography in the New World.

This statement appears reasonably conservative when we recall the figures of the record—the official list of 84,779 baptized on the west coast alone within three decades, and of the magnificent numbers reached after another decade, namely in 1631, of 151,240, the total for the first forty years. If we add to this the missions of the mountains and of the plain country east of the Sierra Madre, which gave additional tens of thousands (the numbers here are not so numerous and there are no official lists available) the total for the first four decades of the mission system must easily, it seems, have passed the two hundred thousand mark. And Ribas carries the story for another twelve years! Indeed, in the final chapter of the *Corónica,* where he sketches the history of the missions up to 1654, he asserts that the records show that four hundred thousand had been baptized since the beginning in 1591.[16] As for territory covered in the Ribas history, it is roughly half as large as the present state of Texas, and for ruggedness of part of it there is scarcely an equal in the West.[17]

---

[15]According to the report of Fray Alonso de Benevides the friars in and about Santa Fe had organized twenty-five missions which included ninety pueblos comprising 60,000 Indians. Cf. Bolton and Marshall, *The Colonization of North America,* p. 243.

[16]The Argentina and Paraguay missions by 1654 seem to have surpassed that number of baptized neophytes. Astrain, *op. cit.,* V, 518, quotes the Paraguayan missionary, Father Francisco Díaz Taño, reporting for the year 1652. He avers that there were then twenty-two reductions containing 43,000 souls, the men for the most part being excluded in this count. But, adds Taño, according to the records more than 150,000 had been baptized, but had subsequently died of the plague or been carried off by the Paulistas, those wild colonists of Brazil, who had destroyed twenty-six pueblos. The missionary quotes the not very reliable authority of a royal *cédula* to the effect that the Paulistas had carried off 300,000 souls and over. But it seems that these were not all baptized. At their height the Paraguay reductions comprised 140,000 Indians and over. Cf. *ibid.,* p. 537. The Jesuit missions of New Spain in 1678 comprised 62,599 Christian Indians. Cf. *Relacion de las Missiones . . . que . . . hizo el P. Visitador Juan Hortiz Zapata, Archiv. Gen. Mis.,* t. 26, ff. 241ff.

[17]Cf. "Expedition Into the Barranca of Río Urique, Sonora", *Life* magazine, issue of September 25, 1950.

Regarding the development of the missions, the events narrated in the earlier chapters of this present biography give an idea of their interesting and instructive details. In the *Los Triumphos* we read of marches and counter-marches; of battles, sieges, and retreats; of Indian uprisings; of robberies and multiform treachery; of arson, rape, and murder; of the pursuit of fugitives and criminals far over hill and dale, far over precipice and crag. We read of floods, plagues, and devils; of sacrilege with the pillage of churches and the desecration of holy things; of priestly vestments worn in bloody riot or in profane bibulous carousal; of liquor drunk from sacred chalice or from martyr's skull; of the sacred Host trampled under foot; of Black Robes' brains spattered on the ground. Ribas tells of the murder of eleven Jesuit missionaries in the West—of Gonzalo de Tapia on the Sinaloa in 1594, of Fathers Pascual and Martínez in the mountains of western Chihuahua in 1632; and of the eight Jesuits slain within five days east of the Sierra Madre in the frightful Tepehuán revolt of 1616.

No need to mention the sweet amenities of Christian grace and gentleness which flowered in moral fragrance among the neophytes. Some of this has already been told in the early chapters of this biography.

But an important feature of this work must now be mentioned. It is the scientific and scholarly value of the *Los Triumphos*. First of all there is the sheer historical value of the book. The history of these missions tells of one of the great frontier advances of the American colonies of the European powers before the period of independence. And so far as North America is concerned it offers an important chapter of the growth and settlement of the West. It was this northwestern mission system which ultimately, during Father Kino's time and after, was carried beyond the present borders of the United States and into the fertile valleys or wide deserts of Arizona; which leaped the Gulf of California and established stations and missions along the thorny backbone of the California peninsula. Nor did the mission system cease its advance even after one hundred and seventy-six years, even after the Jesuits were expelled by King Carlos III in 1767. The Franciscan fathers took up the work and carried the establishments into the

green vales and valleys of Alta California and to the very city and
bay of modern San Francisco. In detailing the first six decades of
such an advance lies the distinct historical value of the *Los
Triumphos*.[18]

The work of Ribas does still another service for science. The
linguist, the ethnologist, and the geographer today consult its
ancient pages. Most important feature in these departments is
Ribas' description of the Indian nations and tribes which come into
the story. His first book, besides giving the background of the
history of Sinaloa, is devoted largely to a discussion of the different
Indian nations of this portion of the west coast of Mexico. Then,
at the beginning of each book, as our historian starts upon the story
of a new group, he offers a valuable description of its people:
their habits as to dress, food, cultivation of the soil, methods of
warfare, and manner of hunting, trapping, and fishing. He speaks
of their grade of savagery; of their religion, their magic, their
barbarous superstitions; their caciques, their women, their medicine-
men, and their state of morality; of their simplicity, their love of
truth, and the nobility of certain groups; of the degradation and
treachery of others; of the fickleness and childishness of almost all.
Ribas tells of the houses they live in, of the work they can do in
weaving or in art. He describes their country—their rivers and
their mountains, their vales and their valleys. The differences
of their languages are indicated though not discussed.

But the narrative reflects the faults of its age. All through the
twelve books, sometimes with a naïveté which moves a smile and
which would provoke the cynic, are his stories of edification—
of alleged miracles, of wondrous conversions, of death-bed repen-
tances, and of demons put to flight. In all of this Ribas is typical
of the seventeenth-century churchman. Conquests over the dark
powers of evil were to him the most substantial and lasting triumphs
of the Faith; and it was the inclusion of such as this which made
his book a matter of edifying reading to many a pious soul in

---

[18]Those who wrote the later anuas sometimes made use of Ribas when
composing the synopsis of annual reports from 1615 to 1649, which was
ordered by General Goswin Nickel in 1653. Here, *anua* of 1632, *Archiv.
S.J. Roman, Mex.* 15, f. 258, Ribas is quoted on the martyrdom of Pascual
and Martínez.

America and in Europe, persons who otherwise would not be interested, perhaps, in the habits of the American savage or the advance of the American frontier.

In the centuries of the Counter-Reformation Catholic writers became prone, among other things equally uncritical, to behold almost anywhere or everywhere the presence and the working of an evil spirit. They became as uncritical with regard to bitter things wrought by the dark powers of evil as they did concerning sweet things wrought by the benign powers of Good. In this Pérez de Ribas was a child of his age. As he accepted too easily the intervention of the Good through miracles, so did he attribute too easily alleged fantastic or destructive happenings to the spirit of evil.

And yet in all this he was not entirely uncritical, nor did he allow himself to be carried away too hastily by conclusions. He investigated with care the alleged miracle of the blood-soaked altar cloths, premonition of the murder of Julio Pascual. So did he take pains to ponder the alleged phenomena caused by evil spirits, destructive demons who were Satan and his imps.

An example of this, his care in the unemotional study of a subject, occurred while he was on the Yaqui River. It will be remembered that among the Yaquis there was a minority opposed to the coming of the fathers. Hechiceros, too, were numerous here. One medicine-man was on the verge of success in bringing about a revolt, so that Hurdaide had to be called for.[19] Ribas here then, on the Yaqui, showed his intellectual quality. He got transported up to him from Mexico City a learned work on magic, of great reputation at that time, a work which rapidly went through numerous editions. Its title translated into English is the following: *Six Books of Research on Magic Divided into Three Volumes.*[20] Its author was the learned Martín Antonio Delrío become a Jesuit in mature age.

Avidly Ribas devoured its pages and he averred that Delrío does not mention a single case of diabolical possession or demoniac interference in human affairs that had not taken place there upon

---

[19]V, 18.

[20]*Disquisitionum Magicarum Libri Sex in Tres Tomos Partiti,* Louvain, 1599. Cf. Sommervogel, *Bibliothèque de la Compagnie de Jésus,* II, 1894ff.

the Yaqui River. But Ribas accepted all of Delrío's assertions as true; Ribas' guide in these matters was as credulous as himself. No one, knowing the age, will be surprised at such uncriticalness. This was the time—the first half of the seventeenth century—when belief in witchcraft was prevalent and when there festered the mad superstition of the sabbat and the cruel procedure of the witch hunt and witch trial. The learned Delrío himself was as uncritical as the rest, as imbued with the superstition of his time, while his six books of magic undoubtedly did their share in helping to prolong the mental disease from which large parts of Europe were suffering.[21]

Concerning preternatural phenomena, one wonders how far Ribas, though trying to investigate carefully according to his wont, was able to get at the exact truth of things. One wonders whether he ever actually observed these alleged phenomena himself or whether he only accepted too readily the word of his neophytes. We fear it was the latter, for nowhere does Ribas say that he ever himself saw these things. And it appears in general from a perusal of the letters and annals of the missions that the fathers generally often accepted too unquestioningly what their Indians told them. The savage was a child; deceit came all too easy to him; exaggeration under the circumstances was the most natural thing in the world: this made a good story and the padre was keenly interested in it.

When our historian narrates that an old woman told him that the devil appeared to herself and companions in the form of dogs and coyotes, toads and snakes; and when he avers that it was well known to the caciques and fiscals that old women danced with devils and flew through the air, he puts too great a strain upon our faith in the truth of these details and we feel that his own faith in the word of the savage went beyond what caution would allow.[22] In other words, he is simply repeating the classical superstitions of a superstitious age; Ribas too fell victim to the witch fever. He might have had surer knowledge from direct contact, but such things are never seen; one only hears of them.

---

[21]Cf. Lea, *Materials Towards a History of Witchcraft*, II, 640ff.
[22]V, 18.

This is a bad sign and the old and classical way of human deception. Early modern Europe and Protestant America went through the stupidity of belief in witches and were guilty of horrible atrocities connected with the punishment of these unfortunates. The *Malleus Maleficarum* was still read and consulted, and the bull *Summis Desiderantes* (Dec. 5, 1484) of Pope Innocent VIII was still exerting a baleful influence. This was the age in which our historian lived and wrote.[23]

An example may be cited to clarify the question. On the Yaqui, the day before a grand celebration for the dedication of one of the churches,[24] a sick Indian already baptized was approached by Satan and a conversation followed. Said Satan: "It's a great pity that you and your parents continue on without procuring any means for your cure." And he gave the sick Indian some herbs to gain his good will. The devil continued: "Tomorrow is a feast. Dance and be merry and I will dance with you." "But don't you see," replied the Indian, "that we shall have to dance in the church. You will not dare to do that, will you?" "Yes, I shall enter and dance visibly before you," was the demon's reply. The following day after the religious procession had been formed and was moving towards the church, sure enough, the sick Indian beheld the demon dancing before him, but as the march approached nearer the church he lost courage and disappeared. No one else beheld the spirit except the sick Indian.[25]

Such was the Indian's story, and Ribas avers that his neophyte was stricken with remorse for having held converse with such a power of evil, which emotion stimulated his will to greater efforts in the practice of a pious Christian life. Ribas accepted this story as he had accepted hundreds of others similar.

But the application of the rules of logic as to the begetting of certitude from the spoken word, in this case as in many of the others, rules out the quality of certitude and classifies the incident as, at best, a thing of exceedingly doubtful character. Unless we wish to take it that the Christian Indian was tempted merely

---

[23]Cf. Lea, *op. cit., passim.* Pope Innocent's bull and the *Malleus Maleficarum* are well known to students of the age.

[24]Ribas does not mention the pueblo.

[25]V, 19.

by the thought of evil and thus in imagination saw the devil fig-
uratively dancing before him. But from the manner in which these
things are told by Ribas, and generally also from the way they are
reported in the annual letters of the missionaries, the fathers
accepted these marvels literally.

The narratives concerning spirits which Ribas relates as happen-
ing among the Tepehuanes on the eastern slopes of the Sierra
Madre are of another color. Here it happens that a spirit begins
to talk from a stone to an Indian medicine-man or wizard, who is
led thereby to take the stone as an idol, to venerate it, to listen
to it, and even sometimes to feed it, leaving corn or beans according to given direction at the spot where the stone rests.

A typical tale can be given here. Father Gerónimo Ramírez,
who began work among the Tepehuanes in 1596, threw down the
idol of an old hechicero and when the padre did not drop dead,
the wizard was astonished and confounded, for he realized that his
prestige with his people would now vanish. This humiliation led
to his conversion and acceptance of Christianity.

Ramírez got from the old wizard his story which Ribas gives
with great prolixity. Briefly it is this: one day when the Indian
was sitting with others a stone rolled towards him and when he
took it up a voice came from it saying that should he keep it and
respect it he would have all good fortune—victory in war, health
and strength for the chase. Gradually the voice became more familiar and began to prognosticate the future. When it prophesied
war the stone would be covered with blood. Sometimes the idol
would disappear and then come back to view, giving to understand
that more honor should be shown it. Later the hechicero began
to feel the evil effects of his sorcery, debility of body, for instance,
and fears of different kinds. But later when at the advice of Father
Ramírez the wizard gave up these evil connections he experienced
great relief of spirit and his fears were replaced with happiness
and joy.[26]

Out in the plains of Coahuila, too, among the Parras missions
demons allegedly scoured over the land spreading terror. One
night the missionary in one of the pueblos heard a voice as of one

---

[26]Ribas, X, 4.

crying for help. The Indians told the padre it was a man possessed of the devil. The Black Robe with a group of his neophytes followed the cries over difficult terrain to a place hollowed out into caves and caverns. Soon they came to a capacious hollow where the devil was wont to appear, said the Indians, in different forms of forbidding aspect, sometimes even clothed in the robe of a Jesuit. Many had died here of fright, they informed the padre, and pointed to a pile of bones and skulls covered over partly with rocks. The missionary was told that on the roof of the cavern, far above the height that any man could reach, blood stains marked the rock, smears of unholy spirits.

The individual whose cries they had heard lay half-dead upon the floor of the cave. All that night he remained unconscious, but next morning he came gradually to his senses. Delighted at his rescue he embraced the Faith and was baptized, which extraordinary event led to a hundred other baptisms. A religious procession was organized to the place. It was blessed and an altar to the true God was set up within it and the cave was christened Santiago, for it was that day the Feast of St. James the Apostle. From that moment the fearsome apparitions ceased.[27]

Ribas is careful to tell us here that he received this story from the pen of the missionary himself, and the story got into the anuas. But here the blood stains are on a cliff, instead of within the cave![28]

There is reason to believe that a certain percentage of these stories may be true in substance. Some or many of them could have had a foundation in actual, if not always visible experience. The persistency with which most of the missionaries tell them is an effect which demands a cause—credulity perhaps?

Again, there is nothing entirely new in all of this. In every age of man, spirits have been in contact with the human race. Mediums of every age have put themselves in communication with the spirit world. Cases of diabolical possession are mentioned in those authentic historical documents, the Gospels, and the history of Christianity is not lacking reliable cases of the felt presence of demons,

---

[27]Ribas, XI, 9. This may well be the cave of Texcalco just off the fringes of Parras which is still a shrine and place of pilgrimage.

[28]*Anua* of 1604, *Archiv. S.J. Roman., Mex.* 14, f. 378.

sometimes of visible form or at least visible by their effects. And the Chinese missionary of the twentieth century will speak of the evident signs of malignant influences.

While a broad philosophy has always admitted the possibility of the intervention of spirits, it will help to remember that the Indians were very close to nature, very close to the soil. Simple and stupid children, they could easily yield their flaccid will and dull understanding to the superstitious and to the mysterious and thus become an easy target for the influence of spirits.

Happily, however, good spirits likewise put in an appearance, like the incident of the baptized neophyte trudging back to his pueblo and being suddenly struck down with fever. "Get up," he heard a voice calling out to him. Looking about he saw a youth —an angel—who informed him the sickness was a punishment of his carelessness in disregarding the instructions of his padre for virtuous living. Then on the instant he was physically cured and spiritually reformed. The neophyte considered, avers Ribas, that this was his Guardian Angel.[29]

Because of the uncritical acceptance of alleged miracles in the sixteenth and early seventeenth centuries in connection with the biographical sketches or lives of reputedly holy persons, Pope Urban VIII issued on October 30, 1625, a bull against the use of marks of veneration with regard to persons of reputed sanctity not yet officially beatified or canonized, such as the placing of a halo about their head. This document likewise forbade the publication of certain events as miracles. Thereafter ecclesiastical writers in their works incorporated a protestation that they had no intention of forestalling the judgment of the Holy See in such matters.

Ribas has this protestation. He knew well that in his relation of the marvelous he ought not to speak of such things as formal miracles. He could and did recount the alleged fact, however, without passing judgment as to its formal or restricted miraculous character.

Our author devotes the eighth chapter of his seventh book to miraculous phenomena. There is no question that he believed these things surpassed the powers of nature and that they were brought

---

[29]V, 20.

about by supernatural intervention. He did not pass formal judgment and he knew he prudently should not and obediently could
not. He says significantly: "It is not my place to pass judgment
as to the authenticity of miracles, for this belongs to higher authority in the Church; but only historically to recount the works
of a divine and singular providence which, more than ordinarily,
has been made manifest in the conversions of these nations."[30]

There is one instance where Ribas is caught squarely at it:
namely, the acceptance of miracle from legendary report, as is
exemplified by the following: Cogoxito was one of the important
leaders of the Tepehuán revolt and after the murder of the priests
and the other Spaniards he with other rebel chiefs and hundreds
of their people fled into the rugged country of the Sierra Madre
southwest of Durango. Governor Gaspar de Alvear in a third
punitive expedition in the spring of 1618 was able to track the
rebel down and to slay him in his mountain fastnesses. Now the
chaplain who accompanied the expedition was Father Alonso del
Valle who gives a long and exceedingly prolix account of the
activities and adventures of the pursuit of the rebels in these
barrancas.[31] Father del Valle tells of the death of Cogoxito. The
rebel trying to escape from a gorge was shot at with bow and
arrow by the Governor's Indian allies and hit three times. One
bolt pierced his throat, issuing on the right side of his neck; a
second arrow wounded him between the shoulders after he had
flung himself from his mount and tried to scramble away; a third
shaft brought him low with a mortal wound. The Spanish soldiers
came running up and dispatched the rebel with his own lance.
Thus the detailed account of Chaplain del Valle who was on the
spot and probably an eye-witness.

Now what does Ribas make of this? After stating that Cogoxito
was overtaken and slain, he says: "The Indians of the ambuscade
aimed principally at this sacrilegious person. Although the arrows
struck him in different parts of his body, the points of the three
arrows came out his mouth in punishment of his blasphemies
which through his mouth he had spit forth when he denied publicly

---

[30]VII, 8.
[31]*Doc. Hist. Mex.*, series 4, vol. 3, pp. 90-129.

the true God and, blaspheming, dared to adore the devil."[32] Evidently, the fact that the first arrow struck the rebel in the throat gave the idea of miraculous punishment to some enthusiastic padre or other Spaniard and legend then began to soar upon swift and ever-increasing wings. The legend sped to Ribas and Ribas, this time incautious, fell.

Ribas does not always, however, lightly pass off such alleged miracles upon the reader. A typical instance of his care and conscientiousness occurs at the end of his fourth book where he is narrating the circumstances of the murder of Fathers Pascual and Martínez at the hands of the Varohíos in the mountains of western Chihuahua. Here, accepting what Ribas writes, a classical miracle occurred: premonition of the martyr's death. And it happened in a classical way: stains of blood about the martyr's person some days before the actual murder.

The phenomena as narrated by Ribas are as follows:[33] a few days before his death while saying Mass, Julio Pascual suddenly noticed after the elevation of the chalice that the corporal and the altar cloths were red with fresh blood. The cloths, corporal, and purificator remained thus stained even after the Mass was over and after the father had returned to the sacristy. Pascual showed the blood-red linens to the boy who had served his Mass, but who had already observed the phenomenon; Pascual showed the cloths likewise to three Indians who were present. The next day the linens had returned to their natural color.

Ribas takes great pains to confirm the truth of all of this, which he does in scientific manner. The three witnesses (the Indians to whom the father showed the cloths) related these details, avers Ribas, to two different missionaries who later came into the country to take the bodies down into the valley of the Mayo. The uniformity of the witnesses' account was noted by the fathers, who made every effort to get exactly the authentic details of the story. The fathers learned that Pascual, the very day of the alleged miracle, made a disposition of his goods as if his end were near. Ribas therefore considers that the miracle was authentic and a premonition of the martyr's death.

---

[32]X, 31.
[33]IV, 10.

All of this sounds satisfactory and it seems as if we might well accept the word of the careful historian. But straightway we begin to doubt, for this case was similar, continues Ribas, to what happened to Father Gonzalo Silveira in the barbarian kingdom of Monomotapa in the island of Mozambique. This missionary received his death notice by suddenly beholding during Mass his hands all covered with blood.[34] Jácome Basilio who was murdered by Tarahumar Indians of northern Mexico in March, 1652, is alleged by the Jesuit, Mathias Tanner, the seventeenth-century hagiographer, to have had a similar experience. As Basilio elevated the Host during Mass It appeared red around the edge and when he placed It on the altar It stained the corporal.[35]

There is more to come. As the future martyr was saying Mass a dove in flight dipped down into the consecrated chalice and splashed its contents over the face of the padre, and onto his vestments and the coverings of the altar. This is alleged to have happened twice within a few days to Gerónimo Moranta, martyr in 1616 among the Tepehuanes![36] Miraculous incorruptibility of body after death is common in Ribas and elsewhere, and we even read of rivers stayed in their onward flow to give a dryshod crossing to the bearers of the padre's corpse.

The repetition of such phenomena provokes skepticism. Like the swarm of bees which honored the lips of eloquent Chrysostoms when they were babes, or the sacred names lisped by infant Gonzagas as they issued from the womb, so too in these missionary annals the appearance of blood upon the future martyr occurs with a repetition which destroys the objective quality of these marvels.[37]

---

[34]Tanner in his biography of Silveira does not mention this miracle, but he notes others—wild beasts passed near his grave with bowed head. Some beasts kept a continuous vigil at the spot. A constant succession of five eagles honored the missionary in the same manner; a succession of birds in red and white plumage sustained a continuous chorus of song! Cf. Tanner, *Societas Jesu usque ad Sanguinis et Vitae Profusionem Militans*, Pragae, 1675, p. 164.

[35]Tanner, *op. cit.*, p. 547.

[36]Synopsis of *anua* of 1616, *Archiv. S. J. Roman., Mex.* 15, f. 373; Tanner, *op. cit.*, p. 475.

[37]Cf. Delehaye, *The Legends of the Saints, An Introduction to Hagio-*

In conclusion, as we do not accept all the stories of Ribas, it does not seem scientifically correct to reject them all. Some of the marvelous happenings which Ribas recounts may have been true in substance.[38]

Andrés Pérez de Ribas, we have then to conclude, was a Jesuit who was possessed of a sound and practical intelligence, broadened by the philosophical and theological training he had received as a younger man, even though his theology be held partly responsible for his witch superstition, while the credulity of his age explains his too-ready acceptance of miracles.

---

graphy, passim. For an extreme example of a holy Jesuit's biography being replete with fantastic miracles, cf. *The Life of Father Joseph Anchieta of the Society of Jesus,* tr. from the Italian, *Vita del Padre Giuseppe Anchieta della Compagnia di Gesu, scritta da un Religioso della medisima Compagnia,* Bologna, 1670.

[38]Ribas has an annoying habit of omitting dates. Moreover, he joins together into one continuous narrative events which were separated by months or even years with no indication of the time-lapse. This is notably true of his account of the conversion of the Yaquis.

CHAPTER XVII

Sojourn in Europe

While Pérez de Ribas was for the third time rector of the Colegio Máximo, the Province of New Spain held its twelfth provincial congregation.[1] This body assembled usually every three years at the call of the provincial. The forty professed fathers who are senior in the Order have the right to sit in this congregation besides the provincial, who is the chairman, and the rectors of colleges. Sometimes the number may fall short as in this meeting where only twenty-seven professed were present. The reason for this shortage was not lack of numbers, however, but the speed with which the meeting was called on January 22, 1643, by the Provincial Luis de Bonifaz, not giving time for the professed fathers living far from the capital to arrive.

Certain weighty matters connected with the Jesuits' relationship with Juan de Palafox, Bishop of Puebla, caused the haste with which this extraordinary congregation was convened. A delegate must be elected and sent to Rome. The fleet would be sailing for Spain in March, and the Provincial wanted the representative to embark at that time.[2]

The representative, called a procurator, was to attend the congregation of procurators in Rome composed of those elected by the various provinces of the Society spread throughout the world.[3] The local congregation likewise draws up one or more petitions, called from the Latin *postulata,* to be presented to the Father General in Rome that he might after consultation either accede to the request of the fathers or refuse it. For instance, in the fifteenth congregation held in 1653 the Mexican congregation asked the General what his desire might be concerning the publication of Ribas' history of the province, since it had been approved by learned men; also these convened fathers requested headquarters

---

[1]Alegre, II, 239.

[2]*Ibid.*

[3]Such are still regularly convened according to the constitution of the Society of Jesus in all the provinces of the Order.

139

to give the final word in order that another of Ribas' works, *Aprecio de la Gloria,* be allowed to go to press.[4]

Ribas attended this present congregation which convened January 31, 1643, by a double title, as a professed father and as rector of the Colegio Máximo. After his return from the missions he had already attended the meetings of several such. As missionary he was not called because of the great distance, and this was the usual practice. In the congregation of November, 1631, which Ribas attended, there was a namesake, Nicolás de Ribas, which may explain why our Ribas is constantly referred to simply as Father Andrés Pérez.[5]

According to the official regulations, the first business was to elect a secretary, which they did: Father Horacios, and his assistant, Father Diego de Salazar. Then, after a recess of a day or two, given to prayer, consideration and consultation, the congregation proceeded to the election of a procurator. And the lot fell upon Andrés Pérez de Ribas.[6]

When the General, Mutius Vitelleschi, heard of this choice of Ribas he was happy. "I am grateful to the Province," wrote he in March, 1644, "for such a move. It is true that his advanced age causes me some worry because of the labors of travel. If this be no impediment, he is for the rest one to be desired in the midst of matters so important."[7] Ribas was then sixty-eight years of age. Indeed, his life was full and important to the end.

Ribas had already been elected procurator in the congregation which met before his provincialate, in November, 1637. Why he did not then go to Rome we do not know. Perhaps the incumbent provincial, Ayerve, stayed him, realizing that Ribas was on the designated list of his successors. But this time he was going actually to cross the seas and to remain in Europe the whole of four years, not returning until 1647.

The decisions and the postulata of this meeting were therefore to be of particular interest to our one-time missionary and pro-

---

[4]*Colección de cartas inéditas,* reply of General Nickel, Oct. 9, 1655. Cf. also Alegre, II, 406.

[5]*Colección de cartas inéditas,* no. 401.

[6]*Ibid.*

[7]*Ibid.*

vincial; and there were other matters of extreme importance, personally and otherwise, which it would be incumbent upon him to attend to.

As to the decisions of the congregation, these assembled fathers gave it as their opinion that there was no need at this time for a general congregation of the whole Society of Jesus to be held in Rome. Such would call for the meeting in the Eternal City of the provincial and two elected representatives from each of the Jesuit provinces. The times were far from opportune, and besides there was really no urgent need to call so important a convocation. "All Europe is at war and the seas are infested with hostile fleets and with pirates," so that the risks of travel overseas would be very great indeed, decided the fathers.

As a matter of fact, the last stages of the Thirty Years War were being fought out and although the great Cardinal Richelieu was shortly before (1642) removed from the scene, the forces which he had created were the dread and almost the ruin of the Hapsburg cousins of Austria and Spain. This very year, 1643, was the year of Rocroi where the French routed the Spanish infantry and wiped out a prestige which had endured ever since the great captain, Gonsalvo de Córdova, had fashioned this instrument for his King, an army which had not tasted defeat for a century and a half. Well might these Spanish Jesuits fear the French also upon the seas. For the Spanish navy had long been in decline and Richelieu had strengthened the sea power of France.

Secondly, thought the Mexican fathers assembled, there was no great need that men from such diverse places and "differing so much at this time in speech, institutions and affection" should convene in Rome. Perhaps the fathers had fear of the animosities which were running strong because of the war, even though within the Society these were by rule and spirit ordinarily kept well in hand in consideration of the duties of religion and of the common good.

Finally, the Mexican Jesuits expressed themselves as possessing full confidence in their present General, Mutius Vitelleschi, who "does well by this province, which success his age and prudence might well assure . . . and", continues the document, "we hope and pray for his long life and vigor in this prudent administration."[8]

No general congregation, then, was the decision of the professed fathers of New Spain, but they did have a postulatum and it had to do with preparing men for the missions. Judging from Ribas' active interest in his former field of labor manifested while he was provincial, we probably would not be far from the truth did we surmise that his was the chief and guiding influence in the adoption of this single request of the present congregation.

The question of the Indian languages had been from the beginning of the province in 1572 an important item in the concern of superiors and the energy of subjects. From time to time the thing crept into the record from the letters of Aquaviva in 1583 to those of Goswin Nickel in 1659. Aquaviva makes the advancement to ordination depend on the knowledge of one or more Indian languages.[9]

Indeed, just eight months after this postulatum of 1643 had been drawn up in Mexico, General Vitelleschi, apparently of his own accord, brings the matter up in a letter of September 30, 1643, to Luis de Bonifaz, successor to Ribas as provincial. The General, replying to the *informationes* for profession, that is reports concerning the fitness of various candidates, prescribes that for this promotion one must be able to teach philosophy and theology in a Jesuit house of studies or, failing in that, be able to hear confessions in an Indian language. The examiners of these candidates must give their verdict under oath. At least two votes are necessary to pass the subject, and the ordeal (for examiners as well as for examined) must last not only throughout the morning, but must include two hours in the afternoon.[10]

While Vitelleschi's letter of September, 1643, touching on Indian languages was in the mails bound for Mexico, Pérez de Ribas as procurator was carrying to Europe a postulatum on the same subject, and when Ribas would return from Rome in 1647 he would carry back with him definite legislation.

---

[8]*Ibid.*

[9]*Ibid. Instructión para que se atienda con mas calor al ministerio de los Indios.*

[10]*Ibid.* Vitelleschi to Bonifaz.

The Mexican fathers say in part (the instrument may have been drawn up by Ribas) : "There diminishes constantly among us the knowledge of Indian languages. Thus it happens that when bishops ask, as they do from time to time, for some one of ours skilled in these languages to go through the towns and villages of the Indians, hearing their confessions and instructing them in the mysteries of the Faith, there is hardly anyone found who is capable of fulfilling this request."[11]

The document now asks the General to issue a strict order that no scholastic be admitted to the priesthood who has not mastered at least the Mexican language sufficiently to hear confessions in that idiom. As a sanction to this law the fathers urge that each Jesuit before his ordination be obliged to pass an examination in one or another of these languages and that the examiners be obliged to give their verdict under oath, as was done in case of the examiners for the profession of the four vows. If there be a sufficient reason for excuse, then the candidate must be made to learn the language after his reception of the priesthood.

Such was the request which Ribas carried with him to Rome, and although Vitelleschi died and it was over a year before a new general could be elected, Carrafa when he came to office acceded fully and enthusiastically to the request of the Mexican Jesuits. His reply is dated June 21, 1646, two and a half years after the request was made, while the fathers had still to wait another year until the answer was brought back by Ribas. After saying he heartily approves the postulatum and after praising the zeal of the Mexican fathers and their interest in this matter, Carrafa accedes to the request. Moreover, he assures the fathers that, by a letter sent to all the provincials of the Americas, he has made a law for the Jesuit provinces of the New World.

Carrafa changes some details of the plan. No one ordained is to be allowed to hear confessions of Spaniards or to preach, or be engaged in the ministry or be advanced to the profession who is not so skilled in an Indian language as to be able to preach and hear confessions in one or other of the idioms. If a student has been prevented from learning such a language before the priest-

---

[11]*Ibid.*, no. 401.

hood, he must learn it after ordination, that is after the third year of probation, this being the most opportune time, and knowledge of a *lengua* will help towards profession counting for one vote.[12]

The papers which Ribas carried to Europe reached Rome before he did and they provoked a final letter of the General written shortly before his death. Vitelleschi in this document complains to Provincial Luis de Bonifaz about certain abuses in the province and seems irritated about them. He speaks of hearing complaints and complaints: there is a lack of union between Creoles and Spaniards, chocolate is taken too often, the Jesuit students go out on visits, the Jesuit rules are not read monthly in the refectory, the account of conscience is not given, consultations are not being held. "Many of such things and others," writes Vitelleschi, apparently ill and irritable, "are found in the memorials of Father Andrés Pérez."[13]

It seems certain Ribas had not yet arrived in Rome even if he had already set foot in Europe. In March, 1645, the Vicar, Carlos de Sangro, speaks of Ribas as not yet being in Rome because of the weighty affairs which were detaining him in Madrid.[14]

We know, of course, what one of these affairs was: the publication of his *Los Triumphos,* which this very year, 1645, and in Madrid, saw the light of day. Ribas was also to beg of King Philip IV new recruits for the Mexican province.[15]

But other matters, still more weighty and for the present far more important, are mentioned by Sangro. Ribas was at the court of Madrid working to adjust matters with the Council of the Indies concerning the accusations and law suits stirred up by a very strong and a very able ecclesiastic.

This trouble, this storm which broke against the Society in Mexico and blew across the Atlantic disturbing the courts of Europe with its violence, is known to history as the Palafox affair, for the principal and compelling figure in this drama was Juan de Palafox, Bishop of Puebla in Mexico. To Ribas while he was still provincial, Goswin Nickel, acting as vicar for Vitelleschi, indited

---

[12]*Ibid.,* Carrafa to Mexican Province, June 21, 1646.
[13]*Ibid.,* Vitelleschi to Bonifaz, March 30, 1644.
[14]*Ibid.,* Sangro to Provincial, March 31, 1645.
[15]*Ibid.,* Vitelleschi to Bonifaz, March 30, 1644.

a letter under date of June 30, 1641. The Provincial is taken to task for having excluded certain professed fathers from the provincial congregation of 1639 for the sole reason that they were alleged to be favorable to the Bishop of Puebla and were going to bring up the affair in the congregation. "If this was the only reason, it was wrong thus to exclude them," concludes Nickel.[16]

This is not the place to write a history of the Palafox affair. The controversy was complex, long drawn out, and at least on one side extremely bitter. For the imprudence manifested by certain Jesuits of the Mexican province, including the mistakes made even by a provincial, the high-born and virtuous Pedro de Velasco, the Mexican province was severely taken to task more than once by General Goswin Nickel, but especially by Vincent Carrafa. The concern caused in Rome is shown by the fact that at least fourteen times this question comes up in the correspondence which we possess between the generals and the Mexican provincials.[17]

It may help to have a brief and running narrative of the famous case. In 1693 a certain canon of the cathedral church of Puebla, Don Fernando de la Serna, made known his intention of giving to the Jesuits of Vera Cruz, as a foundation for their college, an estate or hacienda valued at 60,000 pesos. The other canons—their chief, Palafox, not having yet arrived—officially notified La

---

[16]*Ibid.*

[17]The manuscript sources are abundant in reference to this famous case, whether we take up the anuas, the *colección de cartas inéditas,* or various other kinds of ecclesiastical and civic official documents. Of the printed works the best and fairest narrative is probably that of Father Antonio Astrain, S.J., *Historia de la Compañía de Jesús en la Asistencia de España,* V, 356-411. Father Mariano Cuevas, S.J., has a well-documented account in his *Historia de la Iglesia en México,* III, 283-312. The eighteenth-century narrative of Francisco Javier Alegre, S.J., *Historia de la Compañía de Jesús en la Nueva España,* II, 273-322 and 330-356 is both too pietistic and too partial to the Society. The bias of Hubert Howe Bancroft runs in the opposite direction: *History of Mexico,* III, 116-135. Strongly in the direction of Bancroft go the chapters of Génaro García: *Don Juan de Palafox y Mendoza, obispo de Puebla y Osma, visitador y virrey de Nueva España,* pp. 143-203. An anonymous life in Italian, *Istoria della vita del Venerabile Monsignore Don Giovanni di Palafox e Mendoza Vescovo d'Angelopoli e poi d'Osma* (Firenze, 1773), I, 224-319, runs in the same vein as the preceding two. Of Ribas' narrative we shall speak later.

Serna that he should make over his property with the formal pro-
viso that tithes be given of it to the diocese of Puebla, this under
pain of excommunication. In 1640 Don Juan de Palafox y Men-
dosa came to take possession of his see of Puebla and by a sig-
nificant combination of circumstances to act as administrator of
the archdiocese of Mexico, and to be official *visitador* of the
audiencia. To this power he was able to add in 1642 the supreme
importance of acting viceroy and captain-general of the royal forces,
since he had effected the recall of Viceroy Cabrera y Bobadilla,
Duke of Escalona, with whom he had traveled to the New World.

In 1642 Canon La Serna actually made the donation of his
estate to the Jesuits of Vera Cruz but without the clause that
tithes be given to the diocese of Puebla. When this transpired the
powerful Bishop of Puebla carried out the threat of his canons
and through his chancellor, Juan de Merlo, excommunicated La
Serna. Since the Jesuits together with the other religious orders
enjoyed the canonical privilege of exemption from the tithes, La
Serna appealed to the Audiencia of Mexico, but as Palafox himself was temporarily its chief, he lost his case here. Appealing to
the Council of the Indies La Serna received the favorable reply
that there should be no change in the present state of laws and
privileges.

Palafox now composed and published a work upholding the
thesis that religious orders should not be exempt from the payment
of the tithes. This was answered by a private memorial to King
Philip IV composed in the name of the Jesuits of Mexico by their
former provincial, Francisco de Calderón.[18] In the intervening
time, while officially opposed, personally the relations of the Jesuits
with Palafox were friendly. He manifested towards the Jesuits
of his diocese marks of confidence and esteem, even taking with
him as companion and helper on his official visitations his great
Jesuit friend, Father Lorenzo López.

---

[18]This quarrel is another instance of the centuries old rivalry between the
secular and regular clergy. In New Spain the bishops repeatedly demanded
tithes from properties owned by the various religious orders and they sometimes complained bitterly that their requirements were not obeyed. The
regulars contended that they enjoyed by canon law an exemption from the
payment of this tax. Cf. Carreño, *Cedulario de los Siglos XVI y XVII,*
estudio preliminar.

But early in 1647 (this was the year Ribas was returning from Europe) the gathering clouds burst suddenly into a storm; the remote and official opposition crystallized into an acute and acrid personal enmity. It was Ash-Wednesday, March 6, 1647, in the afternoon, that the Chancellor of the diocese, Juan de Merlo, sent an official notice, signed and sealed by a notary, to Father Diego de Monroy, rector of the Colegio de Santo Espíritu in Puebla and to Father Juan de Figueroa, superior in Puebla of the Indian school of San Ildefonso, that within twenty-four hours the Jesuit fathers should present to the Bishop for his approbation their official licenses for preaching and hearing confessions in his diocese; that until such was done the fathers must abstain from the above activities. If the mandate were not complied with there would be procedure against the fathers before the law.

The Jesuits after consultation decided not to present the licenses they possessed fearing such an act would be an opening wedge for an attack upon their privileges; but they did send two of their number, Fathers Pedro de Valencia and Luis Legaspi, the following day (early in the morning, it would seem) to call upon the Bishop with the view of reaching a friendly understanding.

The two Jesuits were not successful and the Bishop held to his official mandate of the day before. As sermons and confessions would be in order now at the beginning of Lent the Jesuits decided to allow Luis Legaspi to preach Friday morning since the sermon had been announced and he held licenses from Palafox himself, the fathers considering they were thus justified at least for a sermon in their own church, this being one of their privileges. But just as Legaspi was about to ascend the pulpit in the church of the college of Santo Espíritu a second official notification arrived from Palafox, reiterating his demand to see the licenses. Ignorant, as it seems, of the arrival of this document, Legaspi ascended the pulpit, while his superior, Monroy, replied that he would place the matter in the hands of the provincial, Pedro de Velasco, in Mexico City, and the letter went off that very day.

But Palafox, furious at being disobeyed, as he thought, sent a third *auto* that Friday afternoon, demanding again to see the licenses and this time extending the period to twenty days, threatening excommunication were the conditions not complied with. This he ordered his chancellor to make public throughout the city. In the meantime the Jesuits had written to Provincial Velasco, did not present their licenses, but refrained from preaching and hearing confessions.

When the news of the storm in Puebla came to the ears of the Provincial he ordered the Blessed Sacrament exposed in the Jesuit churches and chapels of the capital and special prayers for the appeasement of the Bishop's wrath. Then he came to a momentous decision after obtaining opinions from the Viceroy, from the Archbishop of Mexico, from the Audiencia and other persons of weight and influence. He decided, instead of ordering his men in Puebla to present their licenses, to appoint, according to another privilege of the Society, what were called in canon law *jueces conservadores,* or protecting judges, to study the case and decide upon the action to be taken.

The Dominicans of the capital saved the Provincial embarrassment by offering themselves for this office, and forthwith two prominent men of the Order, Juan de Paredes and Agustín Godínez, were made judges of the case before the law. These men on the second of April rendered their decision and their sentence. Both went against the Bishop and his chancellor, not for demanding to see the licenses, but for the injuries inflicted in the manner of notifying this demand and for the previous injuries done the Order by the Bishop.

Palafox according to this judgment was to relieve the Jesuits of Puebla of all recent exactions and to recall the mandates given them, this under pain of fine of 2,000 ducats for the Bishop, and excommunication for his chancellor. Palafox disallowed the competency of these judges and disregarded their sentence and mandate. As a consequence, on May 27, the judges excommunicated the Bishop himself and got the notice of the anathema affixed to public places in Puebla.

Palafox was not slow in replying. He had already on the sixth of April repaid the compliment to the jueces conservadores by excommunicating them. In May he set up his own college to draw pupils away from that of the Jesuits and he had forbade any one to molest his pupils under pain of excommunication.

But on June 4 he reached the high point of his measures. That evening for several hours he ordered tolled the bells of his cathedral church, the same majestic fabric which now guards the plaza in Puebla. All the town wondered. The following morning the multitudinous bells rang out again, a calling to the townsfolk. They flowed from all quarters into the cathedral and soon had it packed with curious humanity. Within the choir sat the Bishop with all his canons while one of his clergy preached to the people of Puebla loyalty to their bishop. The sermon over, Palafox arrayed himself in full pontificals, and the canons threw over their shoulders black *capa de coros* or copes. Then, lighted candle in hand, the canons marched slowly following their bishop to a low platform covered with mud and placed at the foot of the steps of the high altar.

Palafox again exhorted his people to loyalty and then pronounced sentence of excommunication against the jueces conservadores and against two of the leading Jesuits. The Bishop and canons intoned the 108th psalm which calls maledictions down upon enemies. At its conclusion, following their bishop, the canons extinguished their candles, flung them to the ground, and trampled upon them.

Such was the dramatic crisis of this quarrel carried out in the extreme of true Spanish fashion. The gruesome ceremony over, the wrath of many overflowed the cathedral; the extreme partisans of Palafox issued forth with the cry: *Viva Palafox, el Obispo Virrey.* The public notices of the jueces conservadores were befouled and the windows and walls of the Jesuit houses were pelted with stones and with mud.

Things now evolved acridly to a finish, taking some time. The Viceroy intervened, seeking peace, and sent armed troops to Puebla, while the jueces conservadores moved into the city and Palafox fled! The canons of the cathedral now quieted down, assumed authority, and lifted all threats and penalties from Jesuit shoulders. The city settled down again to normal existence, and the Jesuits did their customary work.

Palafox had fled the night of the fifteenth of June, 1647. His whereabouts remained unknown, but he returned November 27, only to renew the conflict, encouraged in this by two moves from

Europe: Pope Innocent X intervened in the quarrel with a document which Palafox interpreted as a complete victory for himself; and the King seemed to favor him by sending the Viceroy, the Conde de Salviatierra, to Peru and appointing to the viceroyalty of Mexico the Bishop of Yucatán, Marcos de Torres y Rueda, reputed friend of Palafox. The Bishop of Puebla upon the arrival of the papal brief rode up and down the city in his finest carriage followed by a mob of the townspeople celebrating his triumph as issuing from Rome; he launched a persecution against several of his canons who in his absence had most favored the Jesuits; and he wrote strong letters to the Pope recommending the suppression of the Order. Of the canons, two fled to Mexico City while the others were held prisoners and two of these were forbidden exercise of their priestly functions. This was in 1648.

The Jesuits were finally willing to present their licenses, for a severe scolding had been administered them by the General Vincent Carrafa for not having done this at the start, while the Provincial, Pedro de Velasco, had been taken strongly to task for not showing a more submissive and respectful spirit towards a prelate of the Catholic Church.[19] The licenses were presented on October 23, 1648. Palafox approved twelve fathers immediately, but withheld approval of ten, desiring to examine further their fitness. He then proceeded to a public and formal demonstration of absolution of the jueces conservadores from their excommunication and of the two Jesuits, which excommunication he had fulminated against them the previous year.

Finally, sometime in this year of forty-eight the prelate himself received a *cédula* from the King, dated February 6, recalling him to Spain. Palafox departed February 16, 1649, and he was made Bishop of Osma.[20]

The battle now over in the field was continued in the courts, royal and ecclesiastical, until 1652, where ultimately the Jesuits were defeated in both. The bull *Inscrutabili* of Pope Innocent X

---

[19]Cf. *Colección de cartas inéditas,* Carrafa to Velasco, Nov. 30, 1647; Jan. 31, 1648; June 30, 1648, etc. Multitudinous documents on the Palafox affair run through all the archival collections of this period.

[20]He remained here until his death in 1655.

made two things clear: that no member of the regular clergy could preach and hear confessions without a license of the bishop of the diocese, and that since the Jesuits of Puebla did not present their licenses they had no just reason to name jueces conservadores. Therefore the excommunication by these judges of the Bishop of Puebla was pronounced null and void. King Philip IV in an earlier cédula passed substantially the same judgment concerning the naming of the protecting judges.[21]

Thus briefly the Palafox affair. And so far as Ribas is concerned he was variously and even intimately connected with the controversy from the very start. We do not learn, however, that he made any mistakes, except his alleged exclusion of certain fathers from his provincial congregation because he had heard they were going to introduce the matter officially into the meetings. Ribas was the provincial when La Serna made known his intention to endow the Jesuit college in Vera Cruz with the revenues of his hacienda, which was the occasion of the Bishop's initial irritation. In 1641, the year Ribas went out of office, he published an explanation or reply to Palafox on the revenue the Jesuits derived from their property in the Bishop's diocese.[22] The trouble concerning the tithes began the year after his provincialate. Arrived in Europe in 1643 Ribas spent a long period in Madrid attending to the appeasement of the authorities and defending the Society's position; while Ribas was still in Madrid, the Vicar Sangro, acting in Rome after Vitelleschi's death, received a memorial from Mexico telling him of the whole affair as it then stood; and Sangro in the same letter in which he mentions the above says that he is awaiting the *"Papeles* [Reports] of Father Andrés Pérez, in order that with greater light we may act according to what is proper."[23] An anonymous work published in 1652 on the canonical law of the tithe, entitled

---

[21]Astrain, *op. cit.,* V, 395 f.; Cuevas, *op. cit.,* III, 304.

[22]*Respuesta al Illmo. Sr. D. Juan de Palafox, Obispo de la Puebla, sobre la Renta de los Colegios de los Jesuitas de Puebla y Megigo,* 1641. Cf. Sommervogel, VI, 525. Whether his *Respuesta á D. Juan Diez de Calle sobre diferentes asuntos* has to do with Palafox we do not know. Cf. *Ibid.,* 526.

[23]*Colleción de cartas inéditas,* Sangro to the Provincial, March 3, 1645.

Defensa Canonica, is attributed to Ribas, and he would be the logical person to have written it.[24]

His work finally finished at the court of Madrid, Ribas proceeded to the capital of Christendom, where he attended the general congregation of the Jesuits which elected as General, Vincent Carrafa, in January, 1646. Early in 1647 Ribas was still in Spain; late that year he was back in Mexico with thirteen additional Jesuits.[25]

It was this year of 1647 that the Palafox controversy, as we have just seen, reached its most acute stage. If Ribas was not in Mexico for the crisis of March, he arrived not long after, for at the end of November he was placed by the new viceroy, Torres y Rueda, on a committee made up of church and state officials to draw up a settlement acceptable to both sides—this at the suggestion of Palafox himself who had just come back to his diocese.[26]

Soon Ribas would be engaged upon his *Corónica* in which he gave a full account of this controversy and which was considered the first authority in the affair.[27] It was his handling of this explosive matter which delayed and then postponed indefinitely the publication of his crowning work, a history of the Mexican Jesuits.

So then, after four years of absence, Pérez de Ribas was returning to America with a full basket. He had done what he could about the Palafox affair, little knowing that he would run into the worst of the quarrel. He had been successful in obtaining from the King permission for the addition of more men from Europe and some of these were now crossing the Atlantic with him. As official procurator he was carrying back the famous legislation of Carrafa concerning the required competency of Jesuit priests in the Indian tongues. Ribas had already been appointed one of the consultors to the then provincial, Father Juan de Bueras.[28] Ribas in Madrid had witnessed the publication

[24]*Defensa Canonica por la Dignidad Episcopal de la Puebla de los Angeles,* 1652. Cf. Sommervogel VI, 526.

[25]*Archiv. S.J. Roman, Mex.* 4, f. 422, *Supplementum católogi, anno* 1647.

[26]Astrain, V, 386; Alegre, II, 319.

[27]Cf. Astrain, V, 387.

[28]*Colección de cartas inéditas,* Vitelleschi to Bonifaz, March 30, 1644.

of his great book the *Los Triumphos,* and now on his return he was carrying back something else from General Carrafa, a commission to write a general history of all the Jesuit Province of New Spain.

To be one of the four consultors of the province meant more importance and prestige than it did active labor though this kind of prestige counts for little among the Jesuits. The office would be pleasant, too, because his old fellow missionary, friend, subject, and superior, Pedro de Velasco, was on the committee. But the latter commission of historiography, though probably intriguing, was a gigantic task and was to occupy him for almost all of the remaining eight years of his life, until his creative hand was stayed by death.

CHAPTER XVIII

The Pen Drops From Ribas' Hand

It so happened, then, that Ribas had no sooner published one book than he was desired by his highest superior to write another. The General now wanted a history not only of the missions but of the whole province of New Spain, not excluding the missions. The work was destined to be his *Corónica,* crown and chronicle: chronicle of a whole Jesuit province since its inception, crown of his life's work, for he finished it on the brink of the grave. While negotiations were going on for the book's approval the pen dropped from Ribas' hand and his spirit fled from the scene of earthly travail.

Mutius Vitelleschi died early in February, 1645. It took long for the fathers to gather in Rome for the election of a new general, so that the rest of that year Carlos de Sangro was acting as vicar. Sangro's last letter to the provincial of New Spain is dated from Rome December 30, 1645,[1] and the next is from Vincent Carrafa, now elected General, dated January 27, 1646.[2]

The General lost no time in making up his mind concerning the encouragement of further historiography on the part of Andrés Pérez de Ribas.

In a letter of April 20, 1646, to the provincial of New Spain, then Juan de Bueras, we read the following: "I greatly desire that the history of that province be written and I have imposed the task upon Father Andrés Pérez, as upon one of great competence, who moreover possesses the proper knowledge, as is well known, because of the years which he has lived in the province employed for so long a time both as missionary and as superior. His ability becomes particularly apparent in the book which he has written on the history of the missions of Sinaloa."[3] Carrafa goes on to advise the Provincial that he give leisure to Ribas "for so holy a work" and facilitate the task by the appointment of a brother to be his secretary and copyist. Here, therefore, in 1646 is the genesis of the *Corónica y historia religiosa de la Provincia de Nueva España.*

---

[1] *Colección de cartas inéditas.*
[2] *Ibid.*
[3] *Ibid.*

Ribas organized his extensive material according to topical grouping, not according to chronological sequence. As the work was finally completed it consisted of eleven books separated into two parts. Each book contained many chapters and the greater number of these were again subdivided into sections. In the first book we read of the coming of the Jesuits as a group, in the second of the more personal notices of those who came from Spain in the beginning. The third and fourth deal with the foundation of the colleges; the fifth and sixth with other foundations, and of houses founded outside of Mexico—in Guatemala, for instance, and Havana. The ninth book is taken up exclusively with biographies, while most of the books have several chapters on the same subject. Concerning this ninth book it is interesting to note that its twenty-seven chapters, each containing a biographical sketch, deal exclusively with the lives and virtues of lay brothers. The tenth book deals with the establishment of the vice-province of the Philippines, while the eleventh and last takes up the story of the missions from 1644 when Ribas completed his *Los Triumphos* to 1654 when he completed his *Corónica.*[4]

In this *Corónica* as compared with the *Los Triumphos* we have the usual flowing and delightful style of Pérez de Ribas. His critical faculty, however, does not keep to the high standard (for the times) which had been sustained in his *Los Triumphos.* Engaged here in large measure in biographical sketches of prominent Mexican Jesuits, his pietistic penchant towards the edifying and the conscious purpose thus to exalt the good becomes more apparent. In brief, his desire here to edify weakens more than elsewhere his scientific spirit. Then, he succumbs to the age-old temptation of hagiographers, the too ready acceptance of the marvelous, of

---

[4]There are fifty-eight chapters missing from this printed work, most of them being biographical. All of these may be found complete in the manuscript of the Library of Congress. However, from this manuscript three folios have been torn out from Book I which contained all of chapter twenty-six and parts of chapters twenty-five and twenty-seven. Here too, in Book IV, chapter seventeen is missing, but no folios have been torn out. There are other minor discrepancies between the two sets. A copy was made from this Library of Congress manuscript which is now in the Ayer Collection of the Newberry Library, Chicago.

miracles, in the lives of holy men. These sketches are all of a pattern: their poverty was so intense that their gown was worn to shreds before they would ask for a new one; their chastity so austere that they never looked a woman in the face!

To the narration of the famous Palafox affair Pérez de Ribas devotes over fifty of these closely printed pages of the fourth book of part one, grouping the events into fifteen chapters.[5]

Reading today in the year 1950 Ribas' narrative of the Palafox quarrel of three hundred years ago the modern Jesuit critic is moved to the following reflection: that while censors may sometimes be irksome and some types of superiors may be over-cautious, in the present instance both censors and superiors (non-Mexican) were wise in refusing publication of this work, much as certain Mexican censors and many Mexican Jesuits wished it to appear in book form. That the account of Palafox is pietistic and almost insufferably prolix would not have bothered critics of that age in Spain; but that the narrative is far from being unemotional, that it makes use of harsh epithets against the Bishop of Puebla, that it is patently partial to the Jesuits even to the omission of some costly errors made by them—these are the defects which undoubtedly were caught by the eye of the European censors and superiors.

General Goswin Nickel's statement, in arranging for two sets of censors, that by all means "so precious a thing as the truth" be not infringed upon, was well advised for indeed the whole truth does not appear in Ribas' narrative. We have here an excellent example of the disadvantages of being too close to events to judge them equably; and of the wisdom of providing a check, through censorship, upon emotions become too hot from proximity to the fire. Because of his narrative of this affair the manuscript never did get published during his lifetime, nor for centuries to come. It had to wait until 1896.

Another little work fell upon hard times too. The *Aprecio de la Gloria*[6] was bandied about between censors, provincials, and generals for seven years and at that time a decision as to its publica-

---

[5]Vol I, *lib.* IV *cap.* 22-36, pp. 148-206.
[6]Cf. Appendix I.

tion was as far off as ever. "Send the censors' opinion," writes General Goswin Nickel, "and then this permission so long delayed may be given."[7] While this letter was on its way Ribas dropped into the grave and his spirit was able to make a truer *aprecio* than when it was cabined in the flesh. The manuscript never did see the light of day.

But this story is simple compared to the fate of the *Corónica*. During the seven years that the *Aprecio* was being mired in the sloughs of misunderstandings and slow mails over seas, the *Corónica* had been completed. Goswin Nickel speaks of it already in January, 1654, in a letter to the Provincial, Francisco de Calderón. The General says: "Concerning the history of that province which Father Andrés Pérez is composing there come to us various opinions; some praise it greatly, others not so much."

Already, it seems, some clouds had begun to gather. The General is interested and intrigued. He would like to have the Provincial's opinion of the work and wants the Provincial to express appreciation to the author for the immense labor of its composition which is worthy of admiration. "Some have reported that when a portion of the history began to be read in the refectory, your Reverence ordered that the reading be discontinued, doubtless not without cause. . . . I should like the work to be published, though without any content of error or cause of any offense." Goswin Nickel then instructs Provincial Calderón to indicate to Ribas what deficiencies or errors have been discovered in the work that he may correct them. The General wants Ribas encouraged to continue, so that since the manuscript must pass through the hands of the censors it may finally emerge well perfected and polished. "All of us will rejoice at the admirable and exemplary deeds the history will narrate concerning the foundation of that province."[8]

---

[7]*Colección de cartas inéditas.*

[8]*Ibid.*, Nickel to Calderón, Jan. 30, 1654. Thus the letter is addressed. The list in Schmitt's *Synopsis Historiae Societatis Jesu*, col. 555, gives Diego de Molina as Provincial in January, 1654. As a matter of fact Nickel did not know who was acting as provincial, Calderón (who might have died) or Molina, whom he had appointed Vice-provincial, or Real, who should serve in case of death. Cf. letters of Jan. 24, 1655. Unknown to the General, Calderón had been removed from office.

It is a sign of the contemporary interest taken by the Jesuits in the *Corónica* that while it was still in manuscript and even before it was completed some parts were being read in the refectory of one or another community during meal times. And, as usual, opinions differed. Some doubtless were critical because the author did not say enough; some because they thought he said too much. Perhaps the critics were few, but the few when they are critics make a louder noise than those who approve. In any case, some had praised the work highly even to the General, and, be it marked, the General had said only that some praise it "not so much." This may be his diplomatic way of indicating criticism.

Finally, when the work was completed and handed over to the censors these fathers were "in great admiration of the author and of the book," as Nickel informs the Provincial in a letter of January the following year, 1655.[9] Nevertheless, in this case the General wants to be particularly careful and he gives the reason why. The work, writes Goswin Nickel, "contains a long account of the lawsuit which we have had with Juan de Palafox and the author comments on the bull of His Holiness. All of this and the gravity of the matter necessitates that the history be more closely examined and considered." The General has heard too from various sources that in "many parts" it does not hold to the truth.[10]

Evidently opinions still differed, but we can understand well the reasons for the caution of the General. The Mexican Jesuits had made some grave mistakes in the Palafox affair, as we have seen. Moreover they had suffered severely from these troubles so that it would be difficult for them to pass a clear, unemotional judgment.

We can well understand, therefore, and we can admire the prudence of Goswin Nickel in the arrangements he now makes for a more careful evaluation of the manuscript, free from any local feeling or bias. He tells the Provincial that he is sending a copy to the provincial of the province of Toledo in Spain who will appoint censors to study carefully the work again. The Mexican provincial on his part is to gather together all the criticisms which

---

[9]*Ibid.*, letter of Jan. 24, 1655.
[10]*Ibid.*

have been made and to send them on to the provincial of Toledo. The provincial of Toledo after comparing these two sources of criticism and correction will make the final revision "after being able to form a more perfect judgment." "And thus afterwards," concludes Goswin Nickel, "it may be published with greater security and without danger of failing in a matter so fundamental as the truth."[11]

By the time this letter written at the end of January arrived in Mexico Ribas was no longer in the land of the living. The hand of death had placed him far beyond the touch of what pleasure or pain might have accrued to him as a result of the censorship of his *Corónica.* Having lived for a while in the professed house he died March 26, 1655, in the Colegio Máximo, where he had thrice been rector.[12]

Though the author had been removed from the scene, his manuscript continued to be the object of interest and concern. The procurator of the Mexican province, Diego Monroy, was in Madrid as late as January the following year and was instructed to carry the manuscript back to America with him that the work of the final revision might begin by the censors newly appointed according to Nickel's arrangement. Nickel's letter, January 30, 1656, informing the Provincial that Monroy would carry back the *Corónica* for revision, was not received until over two years after the time of writing, namely on March 26, 1658! And this will explain the delay in getting on with the publication of Jesuit books in America when manuscripts had first to be approved in Europe. Then the record falls silent. But the book was never published in that age; Ribas' biased account of a hot quarrel stayed its appearance for more than two centuries.

Successive waves of history, compared to which the Palafox affair was but a ripple, broke savagely over western civilization. Europe was torn with war—the wars of Louis XIV—while a new and secularized mode of thought developed which was to have portentous effects in the Americas. A century after Ribas passed away and when Jansenism and Gallicanism had weakened the

---

[11] *Ibid.*
[12] *Archiv S. J. Roman., Mex.* 8, 275v., and 281v.

Church in France, the *Philosophes* through their acrid criticisms of unquestioned abuses and of an outmoded system loosened the bonds which held Europe to its past.

The Order to which Ribas belonged was attacked and then suppressed successively in Portugal, in France, and in Spain, whither the new ideas had flowed from France through the passes of the Pyrenees. The fabric of the mission system on the west coast, which Ribas had helped so importantly to build, was injured by the expulsion of the Jesuits in 1767. Finally in 1774 by decree of the Pope himself, Clement XIV, the Society of Jesus ceased to have recognized being in the Church.

The American Revolution came and then American independence. Spain's colonies rebelled and Mexico, now free, was torn with civil strife and has been torn, periodically, until the twentieth century revolution.

All the while the *Corónica* was sleeping quietly upon the shelves of some obscure and private room, given doubtless in the care of friends by the departing Black Robes in their fall.

But the memory of these pages did not perish. The Jesuits, resurrected officially as an organization by decree of Pope Pius VII in 1814, returned to Mexico later in the century, but it was not until the end of that, the nineteenth, that one of the manuscripts of the *Corónica* was resurrected and prepared for publication. This copy had been found in Mexico in the library of the scholarly José Maria de Agreda y Sánchez. Though mutilated and missing thirty-five chapters, it was prepared for the press. In 1896 it saw the light of day, published in Mexico City by the Religious of the Sacred Heart.

Another and more complete manuscript copy, evidently done by many different hands, has found its way into the Library of Congress in Washington. This is complete except for the destruction of only several folios. On the outside of the fine leathern binding of the first of the two volumes which are clasped in rawhide, we read the familiar inscription of *volumine* and *legajo* and *lettras y. b.* which specifications run all through the Jesuit anuas as preserved today in the Jesuit Archives of Mexico. Even the hand, so it seems to the present writer, on the cover of this copy is familiar and certain indications would point to the touch of a later Jesuit historian than Ribas, one who carried on his work, Francisco Javier Alegre, expelled in 1767 by King Carlos III.

Be that as it may, the United States Government, through its librarian, knew it had a treasure. The manuscript was handed over to Charles Warren Currier, Ph.D., Bishop of Mantanquas, that it be compared with the copy in Mexico City, while the ancient hand of a naive Yankee has written on a page of foolscap which lies under the cover of the first volume a long and curious eulogy of the work. "In the whole range of historical information," avers this enthusiastic writer, "whether published or in manuscript, it is doubtful whether a more deeply interesting or more intensely valuable work can be found than this." He then tells how the book was never intended for publication, how here Jesuitical methods may be studied in their character of imparting to the popular mind of Spain an aversion to free institutions, and of how the aborigines were argued into submission. But he praises its perfect truthfulness of spirit and thinks it can be of great profit to the government of the United States because of the geographical, institutional, and propagandist knowledge it is able to impart. The Yankee of the nineteenth century exalts the quality but misses the spirit of the Jesuit of the seventeenth.

The man, then, Andrés Pérez de Ribas, Spaniard and Jesuit, subject of this biography, left immortal works behind him. His living flesh lost its lucid spirit on March 26, 1655. He died in Mexico City and there he was buried. His mortal remains have long since mouldered into dust. His soul lives. On the final day of the world's history, concerning a speck of which he wrote so well, the dust of his body will become again organized and luminous through his valiant spirit. Andrés Pérez de Ribas, then immortal, will love his Maker forever more.

APPENDIX I

Carta de la muerte y virtudes del Padre Juan de Ledesma que murio en el Mexico el año de 1636, Mexico, 1636.

Respuesta al Illmo. Sr. D. Juan de Palafox, Obispo de la Puebla, sobre la renta de los colegios de las Jesuitas de Puebla y Megigo, 1641.

Historia de los triumphos de nuestra santa Fee entre gentes los mas barbaros y fieras del Nuevo Orbe, Madrid, 1645.

Corónica y historia religiosa de la Provincia de la Compañia de Jesús de México en la Nueva España, México, 1896.

Aprecio de la gloria eterna de los Bienaventurados, para que Dios crio al hombre, comparandesola con el derramiento de su preciosa sangre. MS.

Respuesta á D. Juan Diez de la Calle sobre diferentes asuntos. MS.

Defensa canonica . . . por la dignidad episcopal de la Puebla de los Angeles, 1652. (Doubtful) MS.

Historia de la Provincia de Cinaloa. MS.

Cf. Sommervogel, *Bibliothèque de la Compagnie de Jésus,* VI, 525f.

APPENDIX II

CHRONOLOGY OF RIBAS

1575   Birth of Ribas in Córdova, Spain.

1602   Enters the Society of Jesus and goes to Mexico.

1603   Novice in Puebla.

1604   Goes to San Felipe in Sinaloa.

1605   Missionary on lower Fuerte River.

1617   Missionary on lower Yaqui River.

1619   Ribas is recalled to Mexico City.

1620   Rector at Tepotzotlán.

1622   Residence in the casa profesa, Mexico City.

1626   President of the Colegio Máximo.

1632   Superior of the casa profesa.

1637   President again of the Colegio Máximo.

1638   Provincial of the Jesuit Province of New Spain.

1641   Third term as president of the Colegio Máximo.

1643   Goes to Europe as procurator of the province.

1645   Publication of the *Los Triumphos* in Madrid.

1647   Returns to Mexico.

1650   Superior again of the casa profesa.

1653   Retires to the Colegio Máximo.

1655   Death of Ribas.

BIBLIOGRAPHY

(Manuscripts and published works used or mentioned in this biography.)

MANUSCRIPTS

The anuas or Jesuit annual letters in five collections:
The Roman Archives of the Society of Jesus.
The Jesuit Archives of Mexico.
The *Archivo General y Público de la Nación*, Mexico City.
The Bancroft Library Collection, University of California, Berkeley, in the Memorias para la historia de Sinaloa.
The Bolton Collection, University of California.

The Ribas manuscript: *Historia de la Provincia de Cinaloa por el Padre Andrés Pérez de Ribas.*

Colección de Cartas Inéditas de los Padres Generales, Jesuit Archives, Ysleta, Texas.

The Hurdaide letters, *Archivo General y Público de la Nación, Historia, tomo 316.*

Letters and narratives concerning Sinaloa, *Archivo General y Público de la Nación, Misiones, tomo 25.*

Archivo General de Indias. Transcripts in the Bancroft Library, University of California.

Archivo General Manuscrito, sin Fecha., Jesuit Archives, Mexico.

Oré, Fray Luís, Gerónimo de, O.F.M., *Relación de los mártires que ha habido en las Provincias de la Florida*, MS. (Cf. below, Geiger, "The Martyrs of Florida, 1513-1616.")

Ordenaciones para el gobierno de las misiones aprobadas por el Visit. Rodrigo de Cabredo, despues de consulta de todos los Superiores de las misiones, 1610; Jesuit Archives, Ysleta, Texas.

Zapata, Juan Hortiz, Relacion de las Missiones . . . que . . . hizo el P. Visitador Juan Hortiz Zapata (1678), in *Archivo General y Público de la Nación, México, Misiones, tomo 26, fol.* 245-249 and published in *Documentos para la Historia de México, series IV, tomo 3, pp.* 316ff.

Bannon, John F., S.J., "The Jesuits in Sonora, 1620-1687," 1946.

PRINTED DOCUMENTS AND EARLY TREATISES

Alegre, Francisco Javier, S.J., *Historia de la Compañía de Jesús en la Nueva España* (Mexico, 1841). 3 vols.

Anonymous, *Istoria della vita del Venerabile Monsignore Don Giovanni di Palafox e Mendoxa Vescovo d'Angelopoli e poi d'Osma* (Firenze, 1773).

Anonymous, *The Life of Father Joseph Anchieta of the Society of Jesus* (London, 1849). Tr. from the Italian, *Vita del Padre Giuseppe Anchieta della Compagnia di Gesu, scritta da un Religioso della medésima Compagnia* (Bologna, 1670).

Arlegui, José, O. F. M., *Crónica de la Provincia de N. S. P. S. Francisco de Zacatecas* (Mexico, 1851).

Bandelier, A. F. and F. R., eds., *Historical Documents Relating to New Mexico, Nueva Vizcaya, and the Approaches thereto, to 1773,* ed. Charles Wilson Hackett (Washington, 1923-37). 3 vols.

Cavo, Andrés, S.J., *Los Tres Siglos de Méjico durante el Gobierno Español Hasta la Entrada del Ejército Trigarante* (Mexico, 1852).

Charlevoix, O.F.H. de, S.J., *The History of Paraguay Containing Amongst many other New, Curious, and Interesting Particulars of that Country, a Full and Authentic Account of the Establishments formed there by the Jesuits, from among the Savage Natives, in the very Center of Barbarism: Establishments allowed to have realized the Sublime Ideas of Fenelon, Sir Thomas More, and Plato.* Tr. from the French (London, 1769).

Delrío, Martín Antonio, S.J., *Disquisitionum Magicarum Libri Sex in Tres Tomos Partiti* (Louvain, 1597).

Dobrizhoffer, Martin, S.J., *An Account of the Abipones, an Equestrian People of Paraguay.* Tr. from the Latin by Sara Coleridge (London, 1822).

Documentos para Historia Argentina, vol. XIX (Buenos Aires, 1927).

Documentos para la Historia de Mexico, 20 vols. (Mexico, 1853-1857).

Humbolt, Alexander von, *Political Essay on the Kingdom of New Spain.* Tr. from the French by John Black (London, 1814).

Institutum Societatis Jesu, Constitutiones (various ed.).

Lettres Édifiantes et Curieuses Écrites des Missions Étrangères, vol. XI (Paris, 1731).

Loyola, Ignatius de, S.J., *Summary of the Constitutions* (various ed.).

Morris, John, S.J. (ed.), *The Text of the Spiritual Exercises of Saint Ignatius* (London: Burns and Oates, 1908).

Tanner, Mathias, *Societas Jesu usque ad Sanguinis et Vitae Profusionem Militans in Europa, Asia, Africa et America contra Gentiles Mahometanos, Judaeos, Haereticos, Impios, pro Deo, Ecclesia, Pietate* (Pragae, 1675).

Urdiñola, Francisco de, "Informatión Hecha por el Gobernador Urdiñola cerca del Estado de la Provincia de Sinaloa," ed. J. Lloyd Mecham in *New Spain and the Anglo-American West* (ed. George P. Hammond, privately printed, 1932).

Venegas, Miguel (ed. Andrés Burriel), *Noticia de la California, y de su conquista espiritual, y temporel, hasta el tiempo presente* (Madrid, 1757; Mexico, 1943-44). 3 vols.

SECONDARY WORKS

Astrain, Antonio, S.J., *Historia de la Compañia de Jesús en la Asistencia de España* (Madrid, 1902). 7 vols.

Bancroft, Hubert Howe, *History of Mexico* (San Francisco, 1883). 5 vols.

Bannon, John Francis, S.J., "Black-Robe Frontiersman: Pedro Mendez, S.J.," *Hispanic American Historical Review,* XXVIII (February, 1947), 61-86.

Bannon, John Francis, S.J. and Dunne, Peter Masten, S.J., *Latin America: An Historical Survey* (Milwaukee: The Bruce Publishing Co., 1947).

Bolton, Herbert Eugene, *Rim of Christendom* (New York: The Macmillan Co., 1936).

Bolton, Herbert Eugene and Marshall, Thomas Maitland, *The Colonization of North America, 1492-1783* (New York: The Macmillan Co., 1925).

Carreño, Alberto María, *Cedulario de los Siglos XVI y XVII: El Obispo Don Juan de Palafox y el conflicto con la Compañía de Jesús* (Mexico: Ediciones Victoria, 1947).

Caughey, John Walton, *California* (New York: Prentice-Hall, 1940).

Charlevoix, O. F. H. de, S.J., *History and General Description of New France.* Tr. by Dr. John Gilmary Shea (New York, 1900). 6 vols.

Christelow, Allen, "Father Joseph Neumann, Jesuit Missionary to the Tarahumares," *Hispanic American Historical Review,* XIX (November, 1939), 423-442.

Cuevas, Mariano, S.J., *Historia de la Iglesia en México* (El Paso: Revista Catolica Press, 1928). 3 vols.

Decorme, Gerardo, S.J., *La Obra de los Jesuitos en México en la Época Colonial, 1572-1717* (Mexico, 1941). 2 vols.

Delehaye, Hippolytus, S.J., *The Legends of the Saints, An Introduction to Hagiography.* Tr. by V. M. Crawford (London: Longmans Green Co., 1907).

Dunne, Peter M., S.J., *Pioneer Black Robes on the West Coast* (Berkeley: University of California Press, 1940).

———, "The Tepehuán Revolt," *Mid-America,* XVIII (January, 1936), 3-14.

———, *Pioneer Jesuits in Northern Mexico* (Berkeley: University of California Press, 1944).

———, *Early Jesuit Missions in Tarahumara* (Berkeley: University of California Press, 1948).

Farrell, Allen P., S.J., *The Jesuit Code of Liberal Education* (Milwaukee: The Bruce Publishing Co., 1938).

García, Génaro, *Don Juan de Palafox y Mendoza, Obispo de Puebla y Osma, Visitador y Virrey de Nueva España* (Mexico, 1918).

Garrighan, Gilbert J., S.J., *The Jesuits of the Middle United States* (New York: The America Press, 1938). 3 vols.

Geiger, Maynard, O.F.M., *The Franciscan Conquest of Florida, 1573-1618* (Washington: Catholic University of America, 1937).

————, "The Martyrs of Florida, 1513-1616," *Franciscan Studies,* No. 18, July, 1936 (New York: Joseph F. Wagner, Inc.). Tr. from Oré's MS., listed above.

Hebig, Marion A., O.F.M., *Heroes of the Cross* (New York: Fortuny's, 1939).

Jacobsen, Jerome V., S.J., *Educational Foundations of the Jesuits in Sixteenth-Century New Spain* (Berkeley: University of California Press, 1938).

————, "The Chronicle of Pérez de Ribas," *Mid-America,* XX (April, 1938), 81-95.

Janelle, Pierre, *The Catholic Reformation* (Milwaukee: The Bruce Publishing Co., 1948).

Johnson, Harvey Leroy, *An Edition of "Triunfo de los Santos" with a Consideration of Jesuit School Plays in Mexico Before 1650* (Philadelphia: University of Pennsylvania Press, 1941).

Jones, Tom B., *An Introduction to Hispanic American History* (New York: Harper and Bros., 1939).

Lea, Henry C., *Materials Towards a History of Witchcraft.* Ed. Arthur C. Howland (Philadelphia: University of Pennsylvania Press, 1939). 3 vols.

Merriman, Roger Bigelow, *The Rise of the Spanish Empire in the Old World and in the New* (New York: The Macmillan Co., 1936). 3 vols.

Orozco y Berra, Manuel, *Apuntes Para la Historia de la Geografía en México* (Mexico, 1881).

Parkman, Francis, *Jesuits in North America in the Seventeenth Century* (New York: The Macmillan Co., 1899).

Priestley, Herbert Ingram, *The Coming of the White Man, 1492-1848* (New York: The Macmillan Co., 1929).

————, *The Mexican Nation: A History* (New York: The Macmillan Co., 1930).

Repetti, W. C., S.J., *History of the Society of Jesus in the Philippine Islands* (Manila Observatory, 1938).

Ricard, Robert, *La "Conquête Spirituelle" du Mexique* (Paris: Institut d'Ethnologie, 1933).

Rippy, J. Fred and Nelson, Jean Thomas, *Crusaders of the Jungle* (Chapel Hill: University of North Carolina Press, 1936).

Rivera, Manuel, *Los Gobernantes de México* (Mexico, 1893). 2 vols.

Sauer, Carl, "The Distribution of Aboriginal Tribes and Languages in Northwestern Mexico," *Univ. Calif. Ibero-Americana,* No. 5, 1934.

Schmitt, Ludovicus, *Synopsis Historiae Societatis Jesu* (Ratisbonae, 1914).

Shiels, W. Eugene, S.J., *Gonzalo de Tapia* (New York: The United States Catholic Historical Society, 1934).

Simpson, Lesley Byrd, "The Encomienda in New Spain: Forced Native Labor in the Spanish Colonies, 1492-1550," *Univ. Calif. Publ. Hist.*, Vol. 19, 1929.

————, *Many Mexicos* (New York: G. P. Putnam's Sons, 1941).

Simpson, Richard, *Edmund Campion, Jesuit Protomartyr of England* (London: Burns and Oates, 1907).

Sommervogel, Carlos, S.J., *Bibliothèque de la Compagnie de Jésus* (Paris, 1890). 11 vols.

Valle, Rafael Heliodoro, *El Convento de Tepotzotlán* (Mexico, 1924).

INDEX

169

THE MONOGRAPH SERIES

178

THE HEFFERNAN PRESS
150 Fremont Street
Worcester, Mass.